THE DOCTOR'S WALKING BOOK

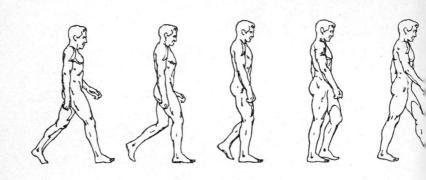

THE DOCTOR'S WALKING BOOK

How to Walk Your Way to Fitness and Health

By
Fred A. Stutman, M.D.
with
Lillian Africano

BALLANTINE BOOKS · NEW YORK

Library of Congress Catalog Card Number:80-81299
ISBN 0-345-28764-9

Manufactured in the United States of America
First Edition: June 1980
  2 3 4 5 6 7 8 9

*"We are under-exercised as a
nation. We look instead of play.
We ride instead of walk. Our
existence deprives us of the
minimum of physical activity
essential for healthy living."*
　　　　　　　—John Fitzgerald Kennedy

CAUTION

Although walking is one of the safest and least strenuous forms of exercise, be sure to consult your own physician before embarking on a walking exercise program.

ACKNOWLEDGMENTS

I should like to thank the following people for their help, without which this book could not have been written: Dr. Suzanne T. Stutman for her editorial advice and editing; Barbara Hillje for her technical recommendations; Joan M. Molz for the preparation and typing of the manuscript; and Ann Birchler, Rochelle Brodheim, Maryanne Johnston, Patricia McGarvey and Linda Wilson for their suggestions and proofreading.

Some of the information included in this book is based on medical abstracts published in *The Physician and Sportsmedicine* (a McGraw-Hill publication) and *Medical Times* (a Romaine Pierson publication), which also supplied the Patient Education Charts reproduced here. Other medical illustrations were kindly supplied by Oxford University Press, Merck Sharp & Dohme, Inc., and USV Laboratories, Inc., and photographs by Camerique Studios, Blue Bell, Pennsylvania, and H. Armstrong Roberts, Philadelphia.

F.A.S.

ILLUSTRATIONS

CONTENTS

THE
DOCTOR'S
WALKING
BOOK

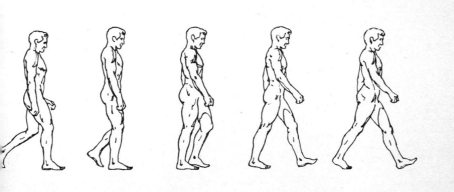

1

WALKING: THE PERFECT EXERCISE

Walking is man's best medicine
—HIPPOCRATES

Let me confess at the outset that I am an avid walker. This book is not like one of those cartoon situations where the doctor advises the patient to quit smoking—with a cigarette dangling from his own lips. Or prescribes a 1500-calorie-a-day diet—while he regularly lets out his own belt a notch or two every few months. In a sense, this book is preaching what I have been practicing for a long time.

I first began walking as a means of escape, a way to get away from artificial lights and into the fresh air. After hours in the office, with nothing but a fluorescent ceiling to light my way, I found it refreshing to take a half-hour walk outside at lunch time, to breathe the fresh air and feel the sun. I found that another half-hour walk in the cool night air was an exhilarating way to unwind.

I'll never forget the feeling I got one winter night, as I walked along the deserted streets after many hours at the hospital. I suddenly realized that I didn't feel cold or tired. All the worries about my

1

patients' illnesses, as well as my own personal cares, seemed to recede with each step. The profound fatigue that I'd experienced as I left the hospital seemed to evaporate into the atmosphere as quickly as the smoky vapor of my own breath disappeared into the winter night. I realized that if walking could have this positive effect on me, then perhaps I had discovered a secret remedy for my patients—one that I was never taught in medical school.

Eventually I discovered more about this perfect exercise. I discovered what it could do for my physical as well as my mental well-being. Not only were my spirits lifted, but my weight and blood pressure were gradually reduced. As I incorporated a regular program of walking into my schedule, I became more and more aware of the benefits others could reap from a similar program. I became so enthusiastic about walking and its potential benefits that I began reviewing all the medical literature (both in this country and abroad) that related to walking and its effects. This book is the result of my own experiences, my clinical observations as a family physician, and my research.

Let me try to convince you to walk your way to better health, a trimmer body and improved fitness.

The Human Body: A Perfect Walking Machine

Walking is one of the most natural functions of the human body. Because of the structure, shape and flexibility of the spine, we are better constructed for walking than for sitting, standing or running.

2

When we sit, the force of gravity exerts a constant pull on the top-heavy head and shoulders, making it difficult for the curved spine to maintain its shape (Figure 1). Subsequently the abdominal muscles relax. This creates more tension on the back and neck muscles—a common cause of cervical (neck) and lumbo-sacral (lowback) pain. We are a little better designed for standing than for sitting, since the bony pelvic structure and the legs can help support the upper half of the body. When we run, however, we pound the ground with a force equal to three or four times our body weight, producing stress and strain on the spine and internal organs.

When we walk, the skeletal and muscular systems perform together—harmoniously. The curved flexible spine is made up of many vertebrae, each separated from the other by a tiny cushion (disc), and has a springlike function designed to absorb shock (Figure 2). These intervertebral discs also give the spine its flexibility and resilience.

The legs are made up of hingelike joints at the knees, ankles and feet. The hips are composed of ball-and-socket joints.

The muscles that attach to the long bones of the legs and the pelvis are specifically designed for walking (Figure 3). The back, hip and leg muscles support the body and propel it forward. The most powerful muscles are located at the back of the hip, the front of the thigh and the back of the leg. The long bones of the leg form a framework of levers to which these muscles are attached.

By a system of contraction and relaxation, these muscles act in unison to move the body forward. The abdominal muscles support the weight of the internal abdominal organs, while the chest wall and diaphragm help us breathe.

3

Figure 1

A midline section of the head and trunk, showing the vertebral column and spinal cord. Note the angle between the fifth lumbar vertebra and the sacrum.

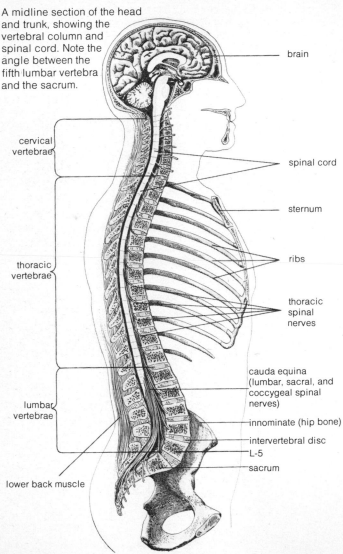

brain

cervical vertebrae

spinal cord

sternum

thoracic vertebrae

ribs

thoracic spinal nerves

cauda equina (lumbar, sacral, and coccygeal spinal nerves)

lumbar vertebrae

innominate (hip bone)

intervertebral disc

L-5

sacrum

lower back muscle

Reproduced by permission of Merck Sharp & Dohme, Division of Merck & Co., Inc.

Figure 2

An enlarged view of part of the lumbar spine and sacrum. The intervertebral discs act as pads or cushions between spool-shaped vertebral "bodies," thus allowing the vertebral column to be flexible. The spinal cord, carrying its myriad impulses to and from the body and lower limbs, lies in a channel behind those "bodies" of the vertebrae and their discs. Bony arches overlie the cord; movable joints are an intrinsic part of the column's flexibility.

Only part of this vertebra (L-1) has been shown, and it has been drawn as if "floating" along with the disk between it and L-2 for illustration purposes.

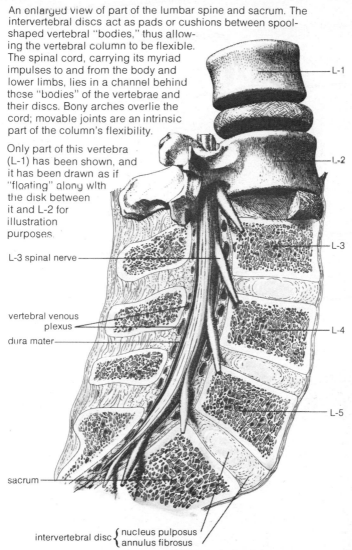

L-3 spinal nerve

vertebral venous plexus

dura mater

sacrum

intervertebral disc { nucleus pulposus annulus fibrosus

L-1
L-2
L-3
L-4
L-5

5

Figure 3
The Hip and the Thigh

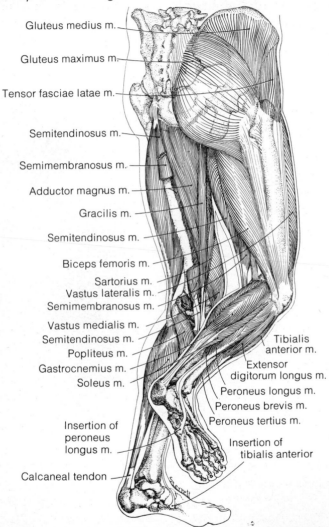

Gluteus medius m.
Gluteus maximus m.
Tensor fasciae latae m.
Semitendinosus m.
Semimembranosus m.
Adductor magnus m.
Gracilis m.
Semitendinosus m.
Biceps femoris m.
Sartorius m.
Vastus lateralis m.
Semimembranosus m.
Vastus medialis m.
Semitendinosus m.
Popliteus m.
Gastrocnemius m.
Soleus m.
Insertion of peroneus longus m.
Calcaneal tendon

Tibialis anterior m.
Extensor digitorum longus m.
Peroneus longus m.
Peroneus brevis m.
Peroneus tertius m.
Insertion of tibialis anterior

The muscles of the posterolateral and posteromedial aspects of the thigh and leg.
Reproduced by permission of Oxford University Press, from *Essentials of Human Anatomy* by Russell T. Woodburne, 1957.

In walking, as the legs swing forward, we are actually catching the forward fall of the heavier upper third of the body. In a sense, we are harnessing Nature's force of gravity. As we walk, we create a near-perfect balance between gravity's pull and this forward motion.

Walking is structurally an almost effortless automatic hydrodynamic process, more beautiful and efficient than man's most advanced machine.

Walking: The Perfect Exercise

Over the years I've compiled excerpts from articles in leading medical journals both at home and abroad pertaining to walking and its benefits.

Studies included in these articles show:

1. Moderate exercise lowers circulating blood fats (serum cholesterol and triglycerides) to the same extent as the more strenuous forms of exercise.

2. Exercise may protect the heart by altering the distribution of different forms of lipoprotein (molecules of fat and protein) in the blood. One type—the HDL fraction—may actually carry cholesterol away from the tissues (the coronary arteries, for example), thus offering some protection against heart disease.

3. People with sedentary jobs run a higher risk of heart attack (coronary artery disease). Walking between 45 minutes and one hour, three or four times a week, may decrease this risk.

4. Walking increases the ability of the heart

and lungs to take in and distribute oxygen in the body. This helps build physical endurance, a factor that has been beneficial to patients with coronary heart disease.

5. A regular walking program, combined with medical therapy, has been helpful in the treatment of hypertension. Walking can lower blood pressure, thus reducing or eliminating the need for drug therapy in some patients.

6. Walking is one of the best ways to get rid of hostilities and reduce tension.

7. Despite popular opinion that exercise increases the appetite, recent data shows the opposite to be true—that regular exercise can reduce appetite.

8. In the village of Lerik, in the Soviet Union, a group of people called the Azerbaijanians have an average life span of well over 100 years. Their longevity has been attributed to regular exercise (such as walking up and down their native mountain slopes), a low-fat diet and a lack of stress.

9. Women who start a regular exercise program can expect the same benefits as men. This is especially important since changing sex roles have made more women subject to stress—and to coronary heart disease.

10. Some researchers say that walking briskly for one hour, five days a week, gives the same metabolic benefits as jogging—without as much risk.

11. For patients who have heart disease and who cannot tolerate maximal-exercise heart rates, a modified exercise program, under a doctor's supervision, can be beneficial.

12. Nutritionists suggest that regular walk-

ing can be part of a lifetime program of weight control.

13. Middle-aged men who engaged in walking, running or bicycle training *all* showed significant improvement in cardiovascular function and body weight.

14. Coronary angiography (visualizing the small arteries around the heart by using dye) has shown that moderate exercise can actually open up narrowed areas in the coronary blood vessels.

15. Walking is now being used in the rehabilitation of patients with peripheral vascular disease (decreased circulation to the legs).

16. In the nonsurgical management of varicose veins, walking, combined with elastic support, is recommended to relieve symptoms.

17. Regular exercise has been cited as one of the factors that decrease the coagulability of the blood and decrease the likelihood of clot formation.

18. Patients with such chronic lung problems as emphysema and chronic bronchitis have improved clinically following a regular supervised walking program.

19. Walking increases the elasticity of the blood vessels, thus decreasing the likelihood that they will rupture under pressure (one cause of strokes).

20. By lowering the resting heart rate and blood pressure, walking helps improve the heart's ability to handle stress, both emotional and physical.

21. Tension headaches have been reported to be successfully treated by walking, as a result of an increased supply of blood to the brain and scalp.

22. The symptoms of some forms of arthritis

can be relieved by moderate exercise, such as walking, when combined with medical therapy.

There have been many statistical studies comparing the incidence of heart disease in population groups with *moderate activity,* as opposed to those with little or no activity. The results indicate that a sendentary life-style seems to increase the risk of heart attack. Many of these studies appeared long before the jogging craze swept the country. The fact remains, however, that no one actually knows what level of exercise is medically the most beneficial. It therefore seems foolish to pursue an unknown level of physical fitness through vigorous forms of exercise (jogging, running, competitive sports) which have inherent risks and dangers.

Walk—Don't Run!

In my years of family practice, many patients have asked me to recommend some form of exercise. My answer is usually: "Walk—don't run." I say this in spite of the fact that running has become the fastest-growing exercise/sport in this country, with some 15 million enthusiasts.

During the past few years, I have been seeing a significant number of patients who have started jogging programs on their own, only to appear in my office with ankle and knee injuries, lowback strains, fractures and other muscle and ligament injuries. These patients were all seeking some way to improve their physical well-being. Many of them were, however, unaware of the hazards.

When you walk, the force of the body on the ankle is about two and a half times your weight. At

10

the knee and hip, the force is about one and a half times body weight. When you run, this force increases markedly, so that any structural weakness or muscle imbalance in the leg becomes apparent. Common running injuries result from muscle overuse and stress on the ligaments. These injuries first produce spasm and pain and may often result in tears in the ligament and muscle fibers. Most involve the knee (35 percent), followed in diminishing frequency by damage to the ankle, foot, shin, Achilles tendon, heel, hip, calf and hamstring muscles. Stress-induced fractures and injuries of the small bones of the foot are also showing up with increasing frequency.

In the course of my research on walking, I also found an equal number of articles which revealed the potential dangers and complications of running as an exercise. Those studies show:

1. Weekend joggers, golfers, tennis enthusiasts, etc. do not develop cardiovascular fitness, because the short bursts of activity are not sustained.
2. "Runner's knee," a form of bursitis, has been reported in approximately 25 percent of jogging injuries.
3. Achilles tendonitis (inflammation of the tendon behind the ankle) occurs in approximately 18 percent of running injuries. On rare occasion, this tendon has been known to rupture, requiring surgery.
4. Muscle injuries, such as pulled hamstrings (a group of muscles in back of the thigh) and shin splints (injured muscles in front of the lower leg), occur in approximately 15 percent of reported injuries.

11

5. Menstrual irregularities have been reported in a significant percentage of women who run.

6. Low back injuries, resulting from excessive stretching of the ligaments and muscles attached to the spine, occur in approximately 10 percent of jogging injuries.

7. The "Type A" personality—the hardworking, aggressive, competitive individual—is approximately 25 percent more likely to develop coronary heart disease. When he engages in a strenuous type of exercise program, such as jogging or competitive sports, he does so thinking this form of activity will lessen his chance of heart disease. However, instead of running off his aggression and tension, he actually runs into it.

8. Heat exhaustion due to salt depletion and dehydration is being seen with increasing frequency in joggers.

9. An increased incidence of osteoarthritis has been reported from chronic joint inflammation, which may result from the repeated use of injured joints during jogging.

10. A condition known as exercise induced asthma has been reported in susceptible allergic patients; this condition promptly disappeared when these individuals stopped running.

11. Heat stroke, though uncommon, has been reported in long distance runners, and if not treated rapidly, can be fatal.

12. Due to the repeated pounding sustained by running, spinal injuries are being reported with increasing frequency, such as herniated intervertebral disc ("slipped disc").

13. Stress fractures of the small bones of the

12

feet are being seen with increased frequency in runners.

14. A recent study has reported a condition known as "jogger's addiction." Individuals who have been instructed to stop running for medical reasons become depressed and manifest symptoms of anxiety. These individuals often resume running against their doctor's orders and often sustain injuries that can result in irreparable damage to their bodies.

15. Recent studies have indicated a new medical complication to jogging: hematuria or blood in the urine. This condition, though benign, appears to be secondary to superficial bruises in the urinary bladder.

16. It was just recently reported that women who exercise vigorously during early pregnancy and who become extremely overheated may possibly run the risk of having babies with central nervous system defects. (This study has to date only been confirmed in laboratory animals.)

17. Nerve injuries of the neck, thigh and leg secondary to jogging have recently been reported. Symptoms range from pain and numbness to actual weakness and paralysis of the muscles supplied by these injured nerves.

18. Long distance runners performing in hot weather develop potassium deficiencies, which if not corrected could result in muscle degeneration.

19. Following strenuous exercise a rare type of allergic reaction has recently been reported. This condition can cause swelling of the face, hands and feet and may result in fainting and breathing difficulties. The cause for this condition is unknown.

20. Many gynecologists feel that since

13

childbirth often weakens the muscular and ligamentous supports of the pelvis, women may be susceptible to prolapse (dropping) of the uterus and urinary bladder during jogging.

21. Extreme exercise, including jogging, can cause sudden death in patients with undetected heart disease. In a recent major city long distance marathon, two cases of sudden death were reported—one while training for the race and one during the actual race itself. Even healthy individuals who have trained properly have been known to sustain heart attacks during excessive physical exertion.

Although many of these reported complications occur infrequently and some are extremely rare, the fact remains that they do indeed happen. One cannot ignore the fact that many of the hazards secondary to jogging are real and are being reported with increasing frequency in the medical literature. With proper precautions, no doubt, many of these complications probably could be prevented or averted; however, it does seem a shame to have to worry about hazards and side effects of an activity that is supposed to be fun and healthful. I think the majority of us would prefer an activity or exercise that is safe, healthful, fun and effective—walking fits this description perfectly.

A recent study in *The Journal of the American Medical Association* investigated the circumstances related to the deaths of 18 people who died during or immediately after jogging. The article stated that although there are health benefits from regular exercise, there seems to be no specific way to identify those individuals who may be risking sudden death during jogging. They further contend

14

that "long-term endurance training and superior physical fitness do not guarantee protection against such deaths."[1] This article contends that further studies are still needed in order to determine which individuals would benefit from endurance exercise as opposed to those who would be subject themselves to excessive risk. This is another startling example of why my basic philosophy is: Walk—don't run.

[1]Thompson, P.D., Stern, M.P., *et al:* "Death During Jogging or Running: A Study of 18 Cases," *Journal Amer. Med. Assoc.* Vol. 242, No. 12: 1265–1267, Sept. 21, 1979.

2
WALKING FOR FITNESS AND ENERGY

Today I have grown taller from walking with the trees —KARLE WILSON BAKER

If you don't exercise, consider yourself part of an ever-shrinking American minority. According to a recent study by the President's Council on Physical Fitness, over 50 percent of adult Americans engage in some form of physical exercise. This is almost twice the number recorded in 1961. The reason?

Americans have realized that health and fitness are not something they can take for granted at any age. They are becoming aware that the things you do—or don't do—today can affect your well-being for years to come.

In the centuries since the first pioneers settled this country, medical know-how has defeated a host of deadly diseases that once claimed thousands of lives. Smallpox, diphtheria and tuberculosis are part of our ancient history.

But as we've softened and refined the rough-hewn quality of Early American life, we've opened up a whole Pandora's box of diseases and ailments that sneak in, unnoticed, along with the benefits of "civilization."

17

As our standard of living has climbed, so has the incidence of heart disease, hypertension, obesity, diabetes, respiratory/circulatory diseases and musculo-skeletal disorders.

Without leaving his bed, modern man can press buttons to turn on his lights, start his morning coffee and turn on his radio or television set. Once up, he can call on another series of gadgets to prepare and cook his food, sharpen his knives, blend his drinks, dispose of his garbage and wash his dishes. If he needs to go anywhere, he can step into a car, a bus or a train.

All of these modern conveniences come under the heading of "energy savers." Presumably all this "saved" energy is used somewhere else—but is it? In fact, the less active person, the one who uses all these machines, has less energy than the man who chops wood, hoes a field and bales hay all day long.

If you find this hard to believe, take an example from your own experience. Have you ever noticed that the less you do, the more tired you are? Or conversely, the more you exercise, the more you have that "raring to go" feeling? The reason for this is that exercise improves the efficiency of your lungs and circulatory system. It increases their ability to take in and distribute oxygen throughout the body.

Since few of us would be willing to move to a cabin in the woods, get up at dawn and grow our own food in pursuit of fitness, energy and good health, we should focus our good intentions on possible modes of fitness.

Although we're bombarded daily with the bad news about environmental factors that can damage and harm us, there is some good news, and this relates to ways we can improve our health and well-being. It's not necessary to quit a job or move to a "natural" environment. It is necessary to make a lifetime commitment to a program of moderate exercise—like walking. If you do, your body will feel the benefits within a matter of weeks.

Oxygen: The Vital Ingredient

Oxygen is the ingredient most vital to our survival. It cannot be stored, so our cells need a continuous supply in order to stay healthy.

Walking increases the body's maximum oxygen uptake, which is a precise measurement of your cardiovascular fitness and your capacity for endurance. It is defined as the greatest amount of oxygen that a person can extract from the air while performing an exercise that uses a large proportion of the body's muscle mass.

When you walk, increased amounts of oxygen are delivered to every organ, tissue and cell in your body, thus improving the efficiency and function of all your body's systems.

Because the lungs have no muscles of their own, they are dependent on the muscles of the chest wall and diaphragm for expansion and contraction. Regular exercise helps condition these muscles to work more efficiently. Exercise also helps to increase lung efficiency by opening more usable lung space for taking in oxygen from the atmosphere.

Studies indicate that regular exercise can actually increase the total blood volume, making more red blood cells available to carry oxygen and nutrition to the tissues. This increased blood volume is also available for the removal of waste products and carbon dioxide from the cells. A second benefit is

19

the increased saturation of the tissues with oxygen; this is probably caused by an enlargement of small blood vessels that supply the individual body cells with oxygen and nutrition.

Walking: An Aerobic Exercise

Exercise can be classified into two categories: anaerobic and aerobic. Anaerobic exercise—such as weight lifting or isometrics—actually impairs blood flow through the muscles. This happens because you are building up tension in the muscles, against heavy resistance. Since the blood flow to these muscles is impaired, fatigue sets in rapidly, and the exercise cannot be kept up for too long a time. There is a relatively low caloric expenditure in this type of exercise, and there are no cardiovascular benefits. In fact, anaerobic exercise can increase both blood pressure and heart rate because of the body's reflex response to this impaired blood flow. Therefore, this kind of exercise can be potentially dangerous, especially for those with a history of high blood pressure or other cardiovascular problems.

Aerobic exercise includes walking, swimming, cycling, running and other active sports. It is designed to increase endurance, and it produces what is commonly called the "training effect." This occurs when the dynamic action of the large muscle groups allows a continuous supply of oxygen through the muscles. By stimulating the circulation in this way, aerobic exercise burns a high number of calories, increases the efficiency of the cardiovascular system, and is thought to be a factor in the prevention of heart and circulatory disease.

When a healthy person complains of shortness of breath, the problem may not be directly related to his lungs. In many cases it means that the heart and blood vessels aren't able to supply the body tissues with adequate oxygen.

Aerobic exercise can solve this problem, but for it to be effective, the exercise must be done continuously for at least 30 to 60 minutes, at least three times a week. While many studies indicate that the heart rate during exercise should be 70–85 percent higher than the normal resting heart rate, other researchers feel that this level is potentially dangerous.

Walking at a comfortable speed may increase the heart rate 40–50 percent above the normal heart rate. This is more than enough to stimulate the lungs and heart and increase oxygen uptake and delivery to all body tissues. The process takes place over many weeks, as the body adapts gradually to the increase in oxygen uptake. According to experts in the field of exercise physiology, two and a half miles of walking will produce the same aerobic benefits as five miles of bicycling, one quarter mile of swimming or one mile of running.

The following study (Figure 4) shows that even though walking is a lower-intensity activity than running, similar fitness development takes place—provided the walking is done more often and for longer periods of time. This chart represents a fitness training program conducted over a 20-week period for men 40–57 years of age. By walking 40 minutes, four days a week, these men showed improvement equal to men the same age on a 30-minute, three days a week jogging program. Notice that the resting heart rate, body weight, body fat and time taken to walk a mile all decreased significantly. The marked increase in the maximum oxygen uptake is shown in the first column.

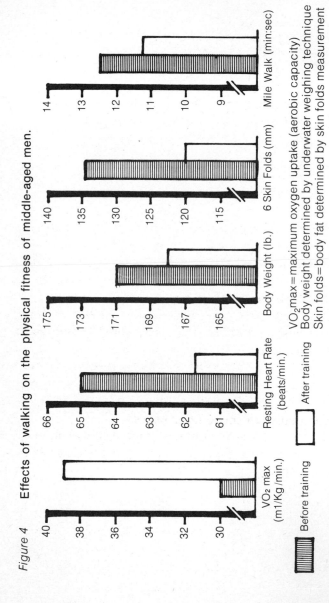

Figure 4   Effects of walking on the physical fitness of middle-aged men.

VO_2max=maximum oxygen uptake (aerobic capacity)
Body weight determined by underwater weighing technique
Skin folds=body fat determined by skin folds measurement

Reprinted with permission of *The Physician and Sportsmedicine*, a McGraw-Hill Publication, from an article—"How Much Exercise is Enough?" by Michael L. Pollock, PhD., June 1978.

22

3
THE LONGEVITY FACTOR

It is vanity to desire a long life without caring whether it be a good life or not
—THOMAS A KEMPIS

We all get old and we all die. But what happens during our lifetime varies enormously from person to person. For some individuals the years after middle age are prime time, an opportunity to relax a little, to enjoy the pleasures of leisure. For others, they represent a gradual withdrawal from life, a downhill slide into physical and psychological misery.

Hereditary factors probably help determine how long you live. But your life-style makes a difference, both in determining longevity and in shaping the quality of those later years.

Recent studies indicate that Americans may be able to increase life expectancy as much as seven to ten years, by:

1. A regular exercise program. The key word here is *regular,* since no exercise will help if it's only done once in a while. A Monday-to-Friday pattern of physical inactivity, followed by three hours of "killer" tennis or squash on Saturday will probably do more harm than good.

23

2. Proper rest and regular sleep habits.

3. Elimination of smoking.

4. Reduction/moderation of alcoholic beverages. Excessive use (and abuse) of alcohol constitutes a serious health hazard.

5. Maintenance of normal body weight. After the age of 35, this may take some added effort, even for people who could once "eat anything without gaining an ounce." After retirement, holding the line may be harder yet, especially for those who leave their jobs with nothing but the rocking chair and the television set to fill the hours from nine to five.

Staying Young

All of us would like to find a fountain of youth—some elixir that would help us to feel and look younger and healthier. In our youth-oriented society, however, we focus mainly on keeping the appearance of youth. Commercials and advertisements suggest—no, demand—that we dye our hair, keep our hands looking young, polish our dentures to a blinding shine and carry on the good fight against crow's feet and wrinkles.

For a fee, plastic surgery will tuck our chins, reshape our tummies and remove any other offending bit of flesh that suggests we might be losing the battle with the calendar.

These choices are fine—as far as they go—if they add to an individual's morale or self-esteem, if they contribute to a zest for living. But it's only recently that we've begun to realize we can do something about the aging that goes on inside our bodies.

The aging process results from a variety of

24

physiological changes. After the age of 30, the heart's ability to pump blood decreases about six to eight percent every ten years. Blood pressure increases a corresponding five to six percent per decade. Circulation also decreases, usually because of a loss of elasticity in the blood vessels, and the accumulation of fatty deposits in the arteries.

With aging, the lungs lose much of their resilience. At the same time, there is a decreased ability of the chest wall muscles to help in ventilation.

The body's muscular system loses its muscle mass at a rate of three to four percent per decade. The result is a decrease of strength and endurance.

All these losses combine to reduce the body's ability to deliver oxygen to the individual cells. Oxygen is the key ingredient for the production of energy at the cellular level. This is referred to as the body's *maximum oxygen uptake capability*. Once this capability is reduced significantly, the aging process accelerates.

If you are inactive, you will age faster. Between the ages of 35 and 50, many Americans tend to become increasingly inactive. The results of this inactivity have shown up in our medical statistics; the death rate from arteriosclerotic heart disease is five times greater in the sedentary population than it is in those who engage in regular physical activity.

Hypertension, obesity, respiratory and circulatory diseases and musculo-skeletal disorders are among the other conditions related to inactivity. We also have good reason to think there may be a connection between the mental deterioration that we call senility and the retirement life-style that is inactive, withdrawn and uninvolved with the world around us.

The not-so-young person who pays attention

only to the mirror and to the gray hairs in his or her comb may become really skilled in the fine art of camouflage. The mirror may eventually tell him that he looks ten years younger, but if he hasn't done anything to help the machinery inside, his bones and muscles and circulatory system may be ten years older than they need to be. He may look youthful enough to join his kids at the local disco. But if he puts his unconditioned respiratory/circulatory system through a couple of hours of "Saturday night fever," he may need mouth-to-mouth resuscitation.

For the sedentary person, there is unfortunately an aging-inactivity cycle. Often the retiree, particularly one who has not had a particularly satisfying job, will look forward to doing nothing, as a reward for the years of endurance. He doesn't realize that this kind of reward is almost certain to make the "sunset years" less vital, less pleasant—and certainly less healthy—than they could be.

Take the case of Joseph, a short, stocky man who had done construction work since he was a boy of 15. As long as he was working, Joseph was an impressive physical specimen. His stamina and endurance were remarkable. He liked to say that he could keep up, in every way, with his three children.

When he retired, Joseph reveled in the luxury of sleeping late and sitting around the house. At first he spent a couple of hours a day doing odd jobs and puttering in the yard. But gradually his day came to revolve around the television set. He became a watcher of soap operas, game shows, old movies—anything at all. To his previous three meals a day, he added an endless parade of snacks—popcorn, potato chips, sandwiches—washed down with beer or soft drinks.

Year by year, the possibilities in Joseph's

26

world got smaller and smaller. The less he did, the less he felt he was able to do. In the first eight years of his retirement, he gained almost 30 pounds. When he developed ostcoarthritis (which, in some form, afflicts some 65 percent of all Americans over 60), this seemed to be one more reason not to move around any more than he had to.

Joseph's loving relatives unfortunately compounded his problem by "helping" him to do less and less for himself. His son and daughters did all his shopping, his cleaning, and even his small errands. They cooked his meals and washed his clothes. Joseph comes from a long line of octogenarians. Heredity and the half-century he spent at hard physical labor make it probable that he will live another decade. But life for him has become little more than marking time. Because of his enormously overweight body—which has become a prison for him—his physical activity has ground to a halt. Though he does little more than sleep and eat, he is always tired, and nearly always depressed.

If Joseph had included one or two long walks a day in his retirement program, if he had been more careful about his diet, he could still have enjoyed the leisure he craved, without the physical and mental debilitation.

In today's mechanized society, we are often programmed to think of physical work as a negative thing. We form habits of letting machines, gadgets and other people do as many of our physical chores as possible. If we used this "saved" energy for pleasurable exercise, the trade-off would make some sense. This is not what usually happens.

Usually, with each labor-saver we acquire, we simply do less. By the time we approach middle age, many of us have fallen victims to the "use it or lose it'' principle, where our bodies are less and less responsive to the occasional demands we do make on them. Because we feel frustrated and strained, we simply give up asking our bodies to stretch themselves at all, and the degeneration continues.

Right now—at whatever age you are—is the time to plan for a healthy retirement. Give your physical well-being as much thought as you give to pensions or insurance. Walk instead of sitting. Walk instead of riding. Walk instead of doing nothing.

In the field of preventive medicine, we have in walking a strong and vital defense against the ravages of degenerative diseases and aging. Walking is the body's built-in mechanism to slow or retard the aging process. It is Nature's way of giving you a tune-up. Use it—now.

The retirement years can be a dynamic, exciting time in our lives, if only we don't give in to those ''retirement blues.'' We can develop a whole new set of ideas and values, with more free time to do the things we've all dreamed about during our working years. This is not a time to stop, but a time to start, to really live and explore the world around us by actually seeing it for the very first time with energy and interest. Walking, then, is our perfect defense against aging, both mentally and physically. Retirement should actually mean to ''re-tire'' ourselves for a new road, a new dynamic life of fun, excitement and activity. The only tires that you'll need will be a good pair of walking shoes (see Chapter 9), and the road beyond retirement will open up for a wonderful, exciting adventure that will last you a lifetime. Walking will make that lifetime last.

4

REDUCING THE RISK OF A HEART ATTACK

Earth and the ancient joy are ever young/
It is the heart that withers and grows old
—JOHN HALL WHEELOCK

Coronary heart disease is the number one health problem in America today. Every year, more than 650,000 people die of coronary artery disease and about 1,300,000 people suffer heart attacks (myocardial infarction).

No age group is immune. About 175,000 people in the above statistics are under 65. However, recent studies have indicated that 72 percent of the deaths in people over 65 are related to coronary heart disease.

In most cases, the cause of coronary heart disease is atherosclerosis of the coronary arteries. This is actually a buildup of fat deposits in the walls of these arteries. The risk factors for this disease include: excessive smoking, obesity, diabetes, high blood pressure, a high cholesterol diet and a lack of exercise. The danger can be reduced by medical treatment and control of these factors. Now we have increasing evidence that a regular exercise program, combined with a low-cholesterol diet, can be a significant factor in both preventing and treating coronary heart disease. Furthermore, if you do suffer a heart attack while you are following this diet-exercise regimen, you are more likely to survive.

Today, physicians have a completely different approach to the rehabilitation of a post-heart-attack patient than they did 15 to 20 years ago. When I was a young Air Force medical officer, I remember being aware of the lack of medical agreement on exactly how these patients were to be treated. At one point, most doctors were reluctant to recommend any kind of activity—let alone an exercise program—for people who had coronary heart disease. So many of these patients were doomed to a life of inactivity and fear—as "cardiac cripples."

As we started to understand better how the heart works, many physicians realized it was important to make our cardiac patients more active.

I remember when it was unheard of to discharge a heart-attack patient before six to eight weeks. That same patient was usually kept at home for another two months before he could resume any kind of activity. Now, patients with the same condition are being discharged from the hospital in three to six weeks, and many are back to work in another four to six weeks. Now, too, doctors are aware of the importance of a regular, low intensity, lifetime exercise program. Ideally, this would be walking.

Coronary Arteries: The Heart's Lifeline

The heart is the body's most powerful muscle. It is actually a double pump divided into two halves by a muscular wall.

The right side of the heart receives unoxyge-

30

nated blood. This is blood which is returning from its circulation through the body, with the oxygen already removed by the tissues. This blood is then pumped to the lungs, where it receives a new supply of oxygen (it then becomes oxygenated blood).

The left side of the heart receives this oxygenated blood from the lungs and pumps it back into the body for recirculation.

The heart must receive its own supply of blood in order to keep working. Oxygenated blood is carried from the largest blood vessel in the body (aorta) through two main arteries that circle the heart (coronary arteries). It is through these coronary arteries that the heart receives its own supply of oxygen and nutrition. These arteries can be blocked by a fat deposit (plaque), a blood clot (thrombus) or by a spasm of the artery itself. This kind of obstruction may cut off the blood supply to whatever part of the heart that artery supplies. If the blood supply remains shut down for any significant length of time, then that section of heart muscle usually dies (myocardial infarction, Figures 5 and 6).

The Framingham Heart Study of cardiovascular risk factors has been in progress for almost 25 years. Using data on more than 5000 men and women, it has provided many statistics on the contributing causes of the major cardiovascular diseases.

Among the causes cited by the study are:

1. Obesity
2. High serum cholesterol and triglycerides
3. Cigarette smoking
4. Diabetes
5. Family history
6. Hypertension
7. Inactivity

31

Figure 5

Resident & Staff Physician Patient Education Chart

Myocardial Infarction—I

What is a Myocardial Infarction? The word infarct means an area of tissue necrosis (death) due to significant interference with blood flow, nearly always the result of occlusion (blockage) of the supplying artery.

Myocardium is the name for the muscular tissue of the heart. It is the contraction (systole) and relaxation (diastole) of the myocardium that comprises the heart beat.

Thus a myocardial infarction means the death of a portion of the muscle tissue of the heart.

If the blood supply is blocked in a large vessel, a large area of muscle can be affected (a so-called "massive heart attack"). If a small artery is blocked, the area affected will be small, and thus the attack will be a minor "heart attack." (The arterial system of the heart is illustrated below.)

Blockage of the artery usually is due to arteriosclerosis (narrowing of the vessel by the buildup of plaque—see inset). This is similar to the narrowing of a water pipe from mineral deposits. The narrowing is not, however, uniform throughout the artery.

See the following page for the areas of infarction produced by blockage of various arteries.

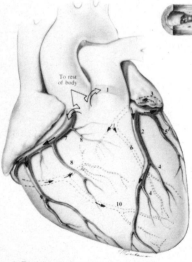

Thrombus
Plaque

Key
1. Left main coronary artery
2. Anterior descending branch of the left coronary artery
3. Circumflex branch of the left coronary artery
4. Diagonal branches of the left anterior descending coronary artery
5. Marginal branches of the left circumflex coronary artery
6. Marginal branches of the left circumflex coronary artery
7. Right coronary artery
8. Right ventricular branches of the right coronary artery
9. Marginal branch of the right cononary artery
10. Posterior descending branch of the right coronary artery

© Resident & Staff Physician 1977
Courtesy of *Medical Times*

32

Figure 6
A Medical Times Patient Education Chart

Myocardial Infarction—II

The most common sites of blockage and infarction are shown here.

Anterior Infarcts
(Infarcts on the front
surface of the heart)

Anterolateral Infarcts
Caused by occlusion of the anterior
descending branch of the left
coronary artery.

Small Anteroseptal Infarct
Caused by occlusion of the anterior
descending branch of the left
coronary artery.

Small Apical (Tip of the Heart) Infarct
Caused by occlusion of the terminal
(end) portion of the anterior
descending coronary artery.

Posterior Infarcts
(Infarcts on the back
surface of the heart)

Posteroinferior Infarct
Usually caused by occlusion of the
right coronary artery.

Strictly Posteroseptal Infarct
Caused by occlusion of the right
coronary artery.

Posterolateral Infarct
Caused by occlusion of the circumflex
branch of the left coronary artery.

Anterobasal Infarct
Caused by occlusion of the circumflex
branch of the left coronary artery.

Posterobasal Infarct
Caused by occlusion of the circumflex
branch of the left coronary artery (due
to variations of vessel distributions).

As you can see from the following chart, the level of physical activity was related directly to the incidence of coronary heart disease.

Table I

Fourteen-year incidence of cardiovascular disease mortality from coronary heart disease according to physical activity

Rate (%) in 14 years

(Ages of men 35–64)

Physical Activity Index	35–44	45–64	55–64	All ages Adjusted
Low Level	3.5%	12.6%	22.5%	12.1%
Minimal Level	4.0%	10.5%	19.1%	10.6%
Moderate Level	1.8%	10.2%	12.0%	7.7%
High Level	1.4%	9.6%	9.1%	6.5%

This chart modified and reprinted with permission of *Medical Times*, Romaine Pierson Publishers, Inc., from an article: "Recent Findings from the Framingham Study," by William B. Kannel, M.D., April, 1978.

As these figures indicate, a person with a low level of physical activity is 86 percent more likely to have a heart attack than one in the high physical activity group. This beneficial effect of exercise did not decline with age.

Still another study, conducted by the California State Health Department and the University of California at Berkeley (and published in the *American Journal of Epidemiology*) followed 3,686 longshoremen over a 22-year period. The men were grouped into three categories—high, intermediate and light—according to the amount of physical energy they used on the job.

During this 22-year period, 395 of the men

died. Of these, 275 were in the light-energy group, 71 were in the intermediate category, and 49 had high-energy jobs. After they analyzed all the available data, the researchers suggested that the difference in the fatality rate could be tied mainly to the difference in physical activity level (although smoking and high blood pressure were also factors).

How Walking May Help to Reduce the Risk of Heart Attack

As modern medicine has developed a better understanding of exercise physiology, we've seen the evolution of many different programs. Among those recommended for cardiac rehabilitation are walking, running, swimming, cycling and selected sports such as golf, tennis and handball.

While these are all aerobic exercises, walking is the easiest and most universally acceptable. It offers the following benefits:

1. Lowers the resting heart rate;
2. Promotes faster return of heart rate to normal after exercise;
3 Decreases the resting blood pressure;
4. Improves the efficiency and capacity of the lungs;
5. Increases the blood's volume and oxygen-carrying capacity;
6. Decreases circulating blood fats;
7. Increases the flexibility of the blood vessels and expands the size of the arteries, including the heart's own coronary arteries;
8. Increases the high density lipoproteins (HDL), which are molecules of fat and proteins in

the blood that appear to exert a protective effect against heart disease;

9. Lessens the chance of blood-clot formation;

10. Improves the heart's maximum cardiac output (total volume of blood expelled from the heart).

All these changes mean that the exercised heart works more efficiently. There is an improved conditioning effect (increased maximum oxygen consumption) that allows the heart muscles to withstand changes—such as a decrease in circulation and oxygen—without suffering the same ill effects suffered by the nonexercised heart. Recent studies also show that a person who has exercised most of his or her life is more likely to survive a heart attack than is an inactive person.

Many exercise programs have shown that sedentary adults can increase their maximum oxygen uptake by 15–25 percent after two or three months. Studies of these programs also indicate that adult men and women of the same age can get the same improved cardiovascular fitness by walking 60 minutes four times a week as they can by running 30 minutes three times a week. These results show that walking offers the same aerobic benefits as more strenuous exercises, without the hazards and the exhaustion.

5

WALKING: AN AID TO CIRCULATION

A man is as old as his arteries
—DR. THOMAS SYDENHAM

Blood Vessels: The Transport System

Blood flows in the following cycle: HEART → ARTERIES → CAPILLARIES → VEINS → HEART.

Once the blood leaves the heart, it is carried through the body by three different kinds of blood vessels: arteries, capillaries and veins. The network formed by these three types of blood vessels is called the *peripheral circulation*. Any diseases that affect these blood vessels are generally called *peripheral vascular diseases*.

Following is a brief explanation of how your veins and arteries work, and how walking benefits both types of blood vessels.

Arteries

As we saw in a previous chapter, the heart acts as a mechanical pump, supplying the force needed to move the blood throughout the body's vast network of blood vessels. First the blood courses through the arteries, which have both elastic and muscular walls that allow them to stretch and recoil as they propel the blood on its way.

Next, the blood passes through the arterioles, the smaller arteries that regulate blood pressure. They accomplish this by actually narrowing their openings in order to control the amount of blood that passes through them (this process is called the *peripheral resistance*).

The next stop is the capillaries, where the blood gives up its oxygen and food to the tissues and receives in turn their waste products and carbon dioxide.

The disease that most often affects the arteries is called *Arteriosclerosis Obliterans*. This condition is caused by the buildup of fat deposits (atherosclerosis) in the walls of the arteries that supply the legs. The fat buildup creates an obstruction in the arteries and results in a decreased flow of blood to the legs. The affected area (usually the calves, hips and buttocks) receives less oxygen as a result of the decreased blood supply. The symptom is pain during exertion (walking, running, etc.), promptly relieved by rest. The condition is called *intermittent claudication pain*. The risk factors for this disease are essentially the same as those for coronary heart disease: smoking, obesity, high-fat diet, diabetes, hypertension and lack of exercise.

Treatment of the disease includes:

1. Treatment and control of any pre-existing illness such as diabetes, hypertension or obesity;

2. Elimination of smoking, since (a) nicotine causes a further narrowing of the artery's passage and (b) carbon monoxide buildup in the blood further decreases the oxygen supply to the legs;

38

3. Proper foot care;

4. Reduction of saturated animal fat and cholesterol in the diet;

5. Possible prescription of medication in an attempt to dilate (enlarge) the arteries;

6. Walking program: a graduated, medically prescribed schedule is an essential part of treatment. Walking helps to dilate (enlarge) the blood vessels near the blocked artery. This is called the *collateral circulation,* and it acts much the same as a road bypass around the blocked artery, enabling blood and oxygen to reach the affected part of the leg.

7. For the 25 percent of patients who do not respond to medical treatment, vascular surgery may be necessary.

Veins

The blood percolates through the small capillaries, where the exchange of oxygen, nutrients and waste products takes place between the blood and body cells. Next, the blood passes through the venules (smallest veins). These join to form the veins, which then return the blood to the heart for recirculation.

By the time the blood reaches the veins, most of the force of the heart's contraction has been spent. This means that the veins (except for those in the neck and head area) have to overcome the force of gravity in order to return the blood to the heart. The return of blood depends on many factors, among the most important are the unidirectional (one-way) valves located along the walls of the veins. These valves prevent the backflow of blood. They are aided by the muscles in the leg (sometimes called the "muscle pump"), which help to squeeze the leg veins and move the blood upwards, back to the heart.

As we walk, the powerful muscles of the legs and abdomen contract and release. They assist in pushing the blood back through the veins by gently squeezing these veins with each contraction (the small valves prevent the blood from falling back down the vein when the muscle releases).

Do you remember feeling faint or light-headed when you had to stand completely still in one place for a long time? This happens because the lower half of your body isn't able to return blood to the upper half without the contraction of your leg muscles to work against the force of gravity. Once you begin to move your legs again, the blood supply to the brain increases, and the feeling of faintness passes.

Prolonged sitting, on a plane or automobile trip, for example—especially with the legs crossed—can slow the circulation down to the point where the feet will swell. Tight-fitting clothes—panty girdles, elastic garters and stockings with tight elastic bands—will cut down the blood flow through the veins. Walking and a few simple exercises (Figures 7 and 8) will correct this slowdown in circulation.

Sometimes, after a patient has had surgery, we see extreme examples of blood pooling. Here, the blood supply in the legs slows down to the point where there is stasis (stagnation of blood) and the possible formation of a clot. To prevent this condition, hospital personnel try to get the post-surgical patient on his feet and walking as soon as possible (early ambulation).

Figure 7

A Medical Times Patient Education Chart

Blood Circulation

Here are some suggestions to help your patients understand—and avoid—circulatory problems while traveling.

During prolonged sitting, such as on a plane or train, your circulation slows down (left). That's why your feet often swell. The blood flow in the superficial veins can also be diminished by constrictive clothing (such as a panty girdle) or by crossing your legs. Relieving constriction (right) will allow venous blood flow to increase.

Simple Exercises to Encourage Venous Blood Flow

Move your foot up and down

Extend your lower legs

Contract the muscles in your abdomen and buttocks

Breathe deeply

Stretch your arms

Close and open your hands

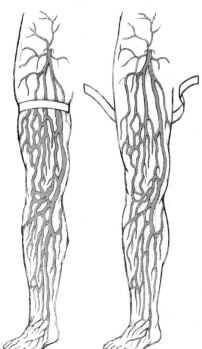

Courtesy of *Medical Times*

© Medical Times 1977

41

Figure 8
A Medical Times Patient Education Chart
Blood Circulation

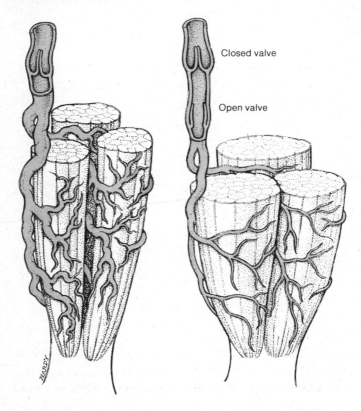

Closed valve

Open valve

During inactivity, blood pools in the veins of the extremities (left). So, if you can, get up and walk around a little. If on an auto trip, make frequent stops to walk a bit. Also, if elastic support stockings have been prescribed for you in the past, wear them on a trip. When the muscles contract (right), as in exercise, the veins are "milked," that is, blood is forced into the larger veins and eventually back to the heart. Valves prevent back-flow.

Courtesy of *Medical Times*   © Medical Times 1977

Another common circulatory problem is varicose veins, which develop mainly in the legs. They can cause pain, numbness and swelling. In this condition, veins lying just below the skin become enlarged, elongated and stretched, so that their valves don't close properly. The result: after the leg muscles squeeze the vein, some blood will flow backwards through the partially opened valve. The amount of blood returned is decreased, circulation slows down and the affected leg may swell.

When you visit a doctor for (nonsurgical) treatment of this condition, he will recommend ways to improve the circulation. These include:

1. Elevating the legs whenever possible;
2. Avoiding prolonged standing;
3. Avoiding tight, constricting clothing;
4. Avoiding the crossed-legs position when sitting;
5. Using elastic or support stockings, in combination with
6. A limited walking program.

Walking therefore can be an effective aid in improving the circulation in patients with peripheral vascular disease. It is also equally effective as an aid to circulation and fitness development in healthy individuals. Walking improves circulation by:

1. Increasing the flow of blood through the arteries by dilating the blood vessel opening;
2. Improving the efficiency of the heart and lungs' ability to take in and distribute more oxygen to the tissues;
3. Assisting in the return of blood by way of the veins to the heart (leg muscle pump).

43

HEALING THE "SILENT DISEASE"

The competent physician, before he attempts to give medicine to his patient, makes himself acquainted not only with the disease which he wishes to cure, but also with the habits and constitution of the sick man —CICERO

Normal Blood Pressure

Blood pressure is defined as the pressure of the blood on the walls of the arteries, produced by the contractions of the heart muscle.

The maximum pressure in the arteries at the height of the heart's contraction is called the *systolic* blood pressure. The lowest pressure, recorded when the heart is relaxing, is the *diastolic* blood pressure.

Insurance companies use the arbitrary figures of 140 systolic and 90 diastolic (which are recorded as "140 over 90" or 140/90), as the upper limits of normal blood pressure. Statistically, the mortality rate rises with persistent pressure readings that exceed this level.

Blood pressure varies somewhat with age, sex and race. It is controlled by:

1. Total volume of blood: this is regulated by the kidneys, hormones and enzymes.

2. Peripheral resistance (resistance to the flow of blood): this is controlled by the elasticity of the large arteries and the diameter of the small arteries (arterioles) and regulated by nerves and chemicals.

3. Cardiac output (total volume of blood pumped out by the heart each minute): this depends on the volume of blood returned by the veins to the heart, and on the force and rate of the heartbeat.

Any condition that interferes with these mechanisms will alter the blood pressure. For example, a lack of regular exercise (which means fewer contractions in the leg muscles) may cause some pooling of blood in the legs. Since a decreased volume of blood will then be returned to the heart, the heart must now work harder to recirculate this blood. This harder work is reflected in a faster heart rate and increased blood pressure. If this lack of exercise persists for any length of time, the result can be a sustained rise in blood pressure.

High Blood Pressure

One out of every five adults—about 24 million Americans—has hypertension, or high blood pressure. Hypertension has been called the "silent killer," since it rarely produces symptoms or early warning signals. Half of the people who have this disease don't know they have it. Every year, this condition is directly responsible for 65,000 deaths, and indirectly responsible for 250,000 deaths from cardiovascular disease and stroke.

Hypertension is actually a misnomer; the disease has nothing to do with tension, personality type or degree of "nervousness." In fact many people with hypertension are neither tense nor nervous.

Hypertension is a disease of the heart and arteries. In 85 percent of the cases, no cause can be found. A diagnosis is made when the blood pressure is consistently elevated for one's age, sex and race. It should never be made on the basis of one reading. However, if your blood pressure is elevated on two or three separate occasions, you probably have hypertension.

People with this condition have seven times as many strokes, four times as much heart failure, three times as much coronary heart disease and twice as much peripheral artery and kidney disease as people with normal blood pressure. In fact, even borderline high blood pressure, left untreated, may triple the risk of strokes and double the risk of heart attacks. Hypertension is the single most important contributing factor in the development of strokes, heart disease and kidney failure (Figures 9 and 10).

For these reasons, it's a good medical practice to have your blood pressure evaluated periodically. Even if you feel healthy, hypertension can be present—and already damaging the brain, heart and kidneys—without giving any warning symptoms. Medical evidence has shown that effective treatment reduces the risk of early death and disability.

At the last meeting of the World Congress of Cardiology, a dramatic decline in the incidence of heart attack and strokes was reported. This was probably due in part to the increased number of controlled cases of hypertension. With proper treatment, a person with high blood pressure can hope for a 35–50 percent drop in the incidence of stroke and heart attack.

Figure 9
A Medical Times Patient Education Chart

High Blood Pressure—I

Hypertension means high blood pressure. It can cause trouble in your brain, your heart, and your kidneys. Blood vessels in the brain may burst and bleed, causing fatal or crippling strokes. You can have a "mini" stroke, which manifests itself by forgetfulness, confusion, fainting, or even incontinence. Hypertension can cause heart disease or be a warning signal of possible future problems. With high blood pressure, your heart has to work harder to supply the tissues of your body with blood—and this imposes a strain on the heart. The small blood vessels of the kidneys are particularly endangered by hypertension. Although damage progresses slowly, a vicious cycle results because kidney disease can cause or aggravate hypertension and the long-term effect on the kidneys may be renal failure. This means that the kidneys can no longer remove waste products and excess water from the blood.

When your doctor takes your blood pressure in the office, let's say he gets a reading of 120/80 on his sphygmomanometer (sfig-mo-man-omiter), the instrument he uses to check it. The first number, 120, represents the systolic pressure, recorded when your heart muscle is contracted. The 80 is the diastolic pressure, taken when the heart muscle is relaxed between beats. Getting to know and understand the importance of your blood pressure and keeping it under control by following the dietetic restrictions and medical regimens prescribed by your doctor can save your life and make your "golden" years more productive and healthier.

The positive thing is—hypertension can be controlled. Your blood pressure can be lowered—but *only* if you follow—each and every day—what your doctor tells you to do.

A "mini" stroke is depicted in this cross-section of the brain. The arrow indicates hemorrhaging of one of the lenticular striate arteries into the internal capsule regions.

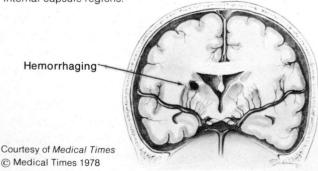

Hemorrhaging

Courtesy of *Medical Times*
© Medical Times 1978

Figure 10
A Medical Times Patient Education Chart
High Blood Pressure—II

Normal Heart

Hypertensive heart shows left ventricular hypertrophy (thickening of the left wall of the ventricle). Left ventricular hypertrophy is a reaction of the heart to high blood pressure.

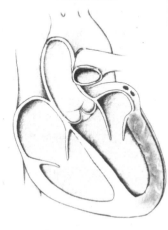
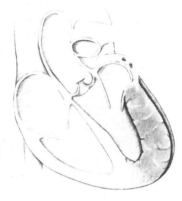

Hypertensive kidney showing constriction of the small arteries of the kidney, and slight shrinkage of the kidney as a whole.

Normal Kidney

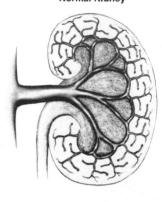
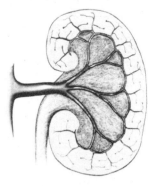

Courtesy of *Medical Times*

49

Preventing Hypertension

Population studies have confirmed earlier reports that people living in areas with a high per capita salt intake have a higher incidence of hypertension. Conversely, those from population groups with a low salt intake (less than 3.0 grams, or two teaspoons daily) have a relatively low incidence of this disease.

A recent U.S. study showed that people who salted their food heavily had a 14-percent higher incidence of hypertension than those who added no table salt to their food.

One effective preventive strategy is to combine a lifetime commitment to a low-salt diet with a walking program. There is increasing medical evidence that a regular program of walking can actually reduce the blood pressure and improve the circulation. Take, for example, a 64-year-old patient of mine, a man with a history of hypertension and coronary heart disease. He asked me if I thought he would be able to jog. I told him I had the perfect exercise for him: walking. At first he was skeptical. Then I explained to him that what I meant was a regular program, beginning with a six-week conditioning program that would gradually build up to a one-hour walk every other day, for a distance between two and three miles.

When I saw him for his next visit, he wasn't completely convinced that the walking was actually helping his physical condition. He did note that he felt more relaxed and that he was having less chest pain. But he attributed the reduction in pain to the new medications I had prescribed for him. I told him to continue the walking program, since he was now completing the conditioning phase.

By his next visit, I found that he was walking two and a half miles every other day, that he had lost six pounds, and that his blood pressure had decreased from 180/100 to 160/90. These changes had been accomplished with no new medication or change of diet. My patient said that he felt much better and had virtually no chest pain at all. Eventually, we were able to decrease the dosage of medication necessary to control both his chest pain and his blood pressure.

A regular walking program reduces blood pressure and heart rate by improving the circulation and making the heart function more efficiently by:

1. Dilating (opening) the blood vessels;

2. Making the blood vessels more elastic and flexible, reducing the resistance to the flow of blood;

3. Improving the return of blood to the heart, allowing the heart to work more efficiently, at a slower rate;

4. Increasing the amount of oxygen delivered to the tissues;

5. Decreasing the amount of catecholamines (this is a group of chemicals which, in high levels, has been associated with high blood pressure) in the blood.

In all these ways, walking helps prevent wear and tear on your heart and blood vessels.

In the field of preventive medicine, the following general recommendations apply not only to hypertension but to many other forms of cardiovascular disease:

1. Have your blood pressure checked regularly by your physician;

2. Take any medication prescribed by your doctor on a regular basis, unless otherwise specified;

3. Eat less salt, sugar and fat;

4. Stop smoking;

5. Decrease alcohol intake;

6. Decrease the amount of caffeine in your diet;

7. Maintain normal body weight;

8. Learn to deal with stress and tension sensibly;

9. Get proper rest and relaxation;

10. Walk regularly.

7

RELIEVING STRESS AND TENSION

Mens sana in corpore sano.
A sound mind in a sound body
—JUVENAL

In my family practice, one of the most common conditions I deal with is tension—which results from some form of stress. Patients sometimes describe it apologetically: "Doctor, I'm not really sick, but I just don't feel as well as I should." Or: "I'm nervous and jumpy." Or: "I'm tired all the time."

Men and women with complaints like these are not victims of some universal microbe. They suffer from the built-in tensions of modern life. They may first experience the milder symptoms of fatigue and nervousness. If unchecked, chronic stress may lead indirectly to peptic ulcers, headaches, sexual dysfunction, depression or other potentially serious conditions. The symptoms of chronic tension have become as serious a problem in our society as epidemics of infectious diseases were in the past.

Our lives are so complicated that we experience stress from many areas: job pressures, money pressures, relationship pressures. Every day, these are compounded by a panorama of minor tension producers: automobile troubles, trains that don't arrive on time, appliances that break down and so on.

Sometimes the steps we take for relief make us feel more pressured than before. We take vacations—and knock ourselves out with schedules for "having fun." We scramble to book a tennis court so we can have the doubtful pleasure of working ourselves into a frenzy over winning. Or we reach for pharmaceutical relief—sedatives, antidepressants, tranquilizers—running the risk of becoming dependent on these medications.

Doing nothing isn't the answer either. It may, in fact, reinforce the feeling of helplessness and depression that often accompanies stress.

One simple, healthy—and habit-forming— way of dealing with stress is simply to get out of your home or office and walk the tensions away. You may have noticed that you feel less tense and better able to think clearly about problems after a long walk. You may have assumed that this was the result of communing with Nature or of changing your environment—in other words, that the benefits you felt were purely psychological. This is only partly true.

The tranquilizing effect of walking is not just in your mind. The feeling of calm has some physiological causes related to the improved oxygen supply and the reduction of carbon dioxide in the blood.

The increased oxygen supply improves thinking ability and memory, lengthens concentration span and heightens clarity of thought.

Recent studies also indicate that exercise may increase the concentration of two different groups of chemicals in the brain known as *endorphins* and *norepinephrines*. These substances appear to have a mood-elevating effect and tend to give a sense of well-being.

For the tense person who also smokes—and this combination can be a killer—walking offers special help. A smoker's blood contains (along with nicotine) an abnormally high level of carbon monoxide, which reduces the blood's ability to carry oxygen. Many smokers find that they can quit or cut down their cigarette consumption after they start a walking program. The exercise decreases the level of carbon dioxide and carbon monoxide in their blood and improves their oxygen consumption. They find their tensions diminishing—along with their desire to smoke.

Along with these physiological changes, there are psychological gains. Walking is fun. You don't have to push your body until every muscle aches and you're gasping for breath. And you don't have to make an appointment or "book" a special place to walk.

Walking is soothing no matter where it is done, but if you can manage a walk in the woods or on the beach now and then, you'll be relaxed by the sense of being at peace (instead of constantly at odds) with the world around you.

By the simple act of using your own legs to propel yourself from one place to another, you feel "in control," not so dependent on wheels and gadgets for every movement you make. The more you walk, the more you can free yourself from life's petty tension-makers: gas lines (and prices), taxi shortages, bus schedules, car pools, and so on.

In a very real sense, walking is Nature's answer to the energy crisis—and to the tension-related health crises that have become part of America's way of life.

Although you can walk anytime—even several times a day—an excellent way to wind down from the stresses of the day is to take a pre-bedtime walk. Instead of popping a sleeping pill, you may find that a brisk half-hour outdoors and under the stars, will bring you home refreshed, tranquilized, and ready to hit the pillow for a sound, untroubled sleep.

THE WALKER'S WEIGHT CONTROL PROGRAM

They have digged their graves with their teeth —THOMAS ADAMS

Obesity is the most common nutritional disorder in America. It affects more than 30 percent of the population, or some 70 million people. Statistically, obesity is associated with premature death and disability from a variety of diseases.

Fat people have a higher rate of hypertension, heart disease and respiratory disorders than do their thin neighbors. As you will note in Chapter 4, obesity is one of the major risk factors in the development of coronary heart disease. Figures 11 and 12 illustrate what happens inside your body when you get fat.

Today, the average American weighs seven to 13 pounds more than he did in 1958, and 14 to 18 pounds more than he did in 1938. With our increasing consumption of rich food and the growing mechanization of our society, we have in a sense created a national problem of excess weight.

An overweight person is defined as one who has been 20 percent or more above his ideal body weight two times or more in a lifetime. The extra

57

Figure 11
A Medical Times Patient Education Chart
Facts About Fat

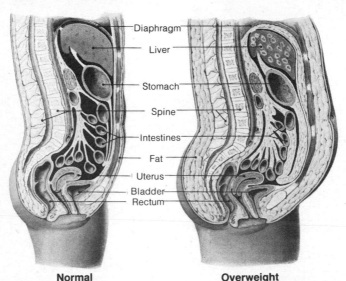

Diaphragm
Liver
Stomach
Spine
Intestines
Fat
Uterus
Bladder
Rectum

Normal　　　　　**Overweight**

If you have a weight problem—controlled or uncontrolled—you are not alone. There are about 15 million Americans who are at least 20% overweight, and that's borderline obesity. The more your weight goes up, the more problems you'll encounter in maintaining health and achieving longevity. "The longer the waistline, the shorter the lifeline" is an all too familiar adage. But sadly, it doesn't really sink in for many people until the insidious growth of girth creates a crisis. This chart shows what happens *inside* your body as you progress from being slightly overweight to being obese. We're not stressing the cosmetic disabilities caused by excess weight—or the psychological problems. We are presenting the gut problem.

Shortness of breath may be a first sign of pulmonary distress and heart strain caused by overweight. The chart shows you how and why obesity increases the heart's workload and contributes to premature death: fat enlarges the capillary bed (tiny connective blood vessels in an area or organ of your body) which increases the amount of tissue to be nourished by the blood

Figure 12
A Medical Times Patient Education Chart
Facts About Fat

Normal Amount of Fat

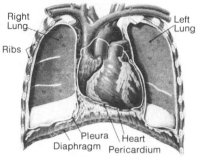

Right Lung

Left Lung

Ribs

Pleura Heart
Diaphragm Pericardium

Fat compressing lungs and heart from side

Excess Amount of Fat

Fat under diaphragm compressing lungs and heart from below

Fat compresses the heart, decreases the blood supply to the intestines, etc. (See figures above.) Some very fat people can't sit, because if they do, there's no space for their lungs to operate in, as the fat invades the chest. These people have to stand up or lie down all the time. They have disabled themselves. Along with all this, extra heavy people—and even moderately overweight persons—are putting an extra burden on their backs and legs (the weight bearing joints), which causes or increases arthritic problems.

Complications following surgery occur more frequently in fat people vs. thin. Wounds don't heal as well or as fast. And again a breathing problem—heavyweights can't take anesthesia as well as people of normal weight.

The final point to remember is that weight will always be with you—as long as you're alive. To control your weight, you have to control the number of calories you eat. Your doctor knows you inside and out better than any far-removed author of reducing plans that please the palate. Your doctor will prescribe a highly individualized diet—just for you—to help you beat the battle of the bulge, which this chart should show you goes on inside as well as out.

and through which the blood must be pumped by your heart.

In addition, the fat accumulated has to go someplace. You can see what's happening on the outside of you—now let's take a look at the inside. Fat infiltrates the liver and other organs. It's a squeeze process, an invasion.

Courtesy of *Medical Times*

© Romaine Pierson Pubs., Inc.

59

pounds do not in themselves necessarily constitute a serious health hazard. But when they are accompanied by other problems—diabetes, hypertension, cigarette smoking or an inactive lifestyle—then the risk becomes more serious. For those who take comfort in "just" being overweight, it should be mentioned that few people over 35 are merely obese; many may also have one or more of the conditions and habits mentioned above.

For them, weight reduction is a health imperative, as it is for people who have hypertension (here, weight loss alone may often be effective treatment for mild cases). Obesity is generally more than a number on a scale. It is usually a way of life—and not a particularly healthy one.

Of course, there are probably millions of Americans who want to reduce their weight for aesthetic reasons. Ironically, during the same period that technology has made us fatter, we have evolved a national attitude that "thin is beautiful."

So, whether it be for health or beauty, we have a billion-dollar industry catering to our physical and psychological need for trimmer, more slender bodies. Because it is the American way to want everything fast, the results have not always been beneficial.

For countless tens of thousands in search of narrow waists and hollow cheekbones, the magic word has been "fast"—or "quick" or "instant." Drawn by such terms as "revolutionary" or "miraculous," they try fruit diets, water diets, low-carbohydrate diets, protein powders and so on.

The majority of these "miracle" methods have one thing in common. They take no notice of the nutritional requirements and health of the dieter.

They fail to explain that any diet which restricts one or more food groups, while increasing amounts of another, is nutritionally unsound.

Playing around with food balances can cause headaches, dizziness, weakness, dehydration, menstrual irregularities, muscle cramps, hair loss, dry skin, vitamin deficiencies or other forms of nutritional depletion. Some more serious conditions associated with fad diets are elevated blood fats and blood sugar, depression, liver and kidney disorders, gout. The Food and Drug Administration is currently investigating a number of deaths that have apparently followed the use of protein powders combined with total fasting diets.

Fortunately, the nutritional damage done by most fad diets is temporary—simply because people don't stay on them very long before they move on to the next "miracle."

It isn't really that difficult to lose ten pounds or so on any one of these regimens. The bad news is that these pounds almost always return—often with interest. Crash diets that result in quick weight loss are usually followed by what is known as the "rebound phenomenon" or the "yo-yo syndrome." This means that the patient is constantly losing and regaining pounds (often more pounds than the original amount lost). This pattern is not only psychologically demoralizing; it can create health hazards (such as stresses on the cardiovascular system) that are more serious than the excess weight.

Many of my patients are on a "forever" diet, losing and regaining enough weight to create another whole person. This usually happens because would-be "skinnies" focus on trying to live without food—when basically they need to learn to live with it—every year of their lives. The failure to understand this is the major cause of dieting frustration.

Although it may not sound like the "American way," the only way to change your figure permanently is to retrain your eating and exercise habits—permanently.

Although every issue of every beauty magazine offers dieting shortcuts, there is one basic equation that is inescapable. How do your "calories in" compare with your "calories out"? A sensible, successful plan attacks this equation at both ends. First, a rational, healthful modification of the "calories in," and next, a walking program to increase the "calories out."

For those who are "out of shape," but not terribly overweight, walking alone may be the ideal choice.

Body-shaping by Walking

Most doctors probably see as many exercise droputs as they do diet dropouts, because the program they choose is either too strenuous or too complicated. I remember one young woman who went from exercise to exercise the way some people jump from diet to diet, starting out with great bursts of enthusiasm, but giving up when the exercise required sustained effort on her part.

Helen has a desk job. She is in good health and well within the "ideal" weight range for her height. Her complaint: the tops of her legs are too heavy, and her figure is "mushy." For Helen, dieting would not be a solution, since she'd have to reduce to the point of emaciation to achieve the kind of body-shaping she wants.

For her, exercise is the way to go. Helen's first choice was a group of ten-minutes-a-day exercises, all perfectly good, designed to firm and tone. But after a few weeks, she dropped these because they were "too much work."

When running started to become popular, Helen immediately saw some of the figure improvements in her friends who jogged. So she bought herself a warmup suit and some expensive shoes. On her first day, she covered the equivalent of two city blocks, and came back red in the face and panting. After two more tries, she gave up.

Next came a health spa, where she could swim and use the various exercise machines (many of dubious value). Again, she made an auspicious beginning, but Helen found that her busy work schedule didn't allow for regular use of the spa facilities, and that once again her exercise program was too much like work to be a successful part of her normal life.

I suggested that walking might be the answer. Since Helen is an early riser, I suggested she walk the mile or so from her apartment to her downtown office. She could, I said, get the figure benefits she wanted, spare her nervous system the morning and evening rush-hour traffic, and save a fortune in parking fees.

At first she resisted, especially when she heard that it would take at least a month before she would begin to see some results. "What do you have to lose?" I asked. "The worst that can happen is that you'll save money on gas and parking fees."

After six months, Helen is still walking. She has dropped one dress size, her abdomen is firmer and flatter, and her thighs have lost the "doughy" look she hated.

The Walker's Weight Loss/Body Toning Program is easy, and as painless as any program can be. It is not fast. You will not see miracles in one week. But you will probably not backslide, and you will not grit your teeth while you try to get the program "over with."

The Walker's Plan is fun. And once you establish your new exercise patterns, you will feel—and look—so much better that you wouldn't think of slipping back into a sedentary slump. Those with considerable weight problems may want to follow the two-step program: regular walking combined with simplified diet.

First, let's understand what happens as you begin a walking program:

1. Walking decreases your appetite.
2. Walking burns calories.

If the first statement surprises you, then you may have harbored a common misconception (probably started by people who spend their time eating taco chips in front of the television set) that exercise is bad for dieters because it increases the appetite and makes you eat more. Right? Wrong.

Animal and human studies have shown that regular exercise can actually decrease the appetite. Why? It has been suggested that:

1. Exercise regulates your appestat (the brain center that controls appetite);
2. It redirects the blood flow away from the digestive tract;
3. It stimulates the utilization of blood fats, instead of blood sugar, by the muscles.

This drop in appetite is a great bonus for the dieter. Without the aid of pills or other artificial aids, he/she can take a walk before meals and experience a natural desire to eat less.

How Walking Burns Calories

The following chart can give you an idea of how much energy is expended—how many calories burned per hour—when you walk.

Table II

Walking pace	Calories/minute	Calories/hour
Slow pace (2 mph)	4–5	240–300
Moderate pace (3 mph)	5–6	300–360
Fast pace (4 mph)	6–7	360–420

It takes about 3500 calories to either gain or lose one pound. You can see that a one-hour walk at a moderate pace will burn up 300–360 calories per hour.

Using the suggested program of one hour, every other day, you will burn up about 1400 calories per week (4 hours x 350 calories per hour). This represents an average loss of 200 calories per day.

The following examples will show you how walking at a moderate pace (3 mph) can affect your weight, provided there is no change in your daily intake of food.

Plan 1: It will take 10 hours of walking at a moderate pace (3 mph) to burn up 3500 calories. You can lose one pound every two and a half weeks, using the every-other-day schedule (4 hours per week x 2.5 weeks = 10 hours walking x 350 calories per hour = 3500 calories = one pound).

Plan 2: If you would like to lose weight at a faster rate, you can walk one hour every day and

65

burn up 350 calories daily. Since it takes 3500 calories to lose one pound, you can now lose one pound every ten days, or three pounds a month, or 36 pounds a year.

Plan 3: If you are satisfied with your present weight, then you can be allowed a 200-calorie bonus every day. As long as you continue your one-hour-every-other-day walking (1400 calories expended per week), you can add 200 calories daily to your maintenance diet, without gaining any weight.

Obviously the rate of walking (Table II) will change the weight-loss pattern. The three examples given above are based on the moderate (3 mph) pace. Walking fast (4 mph) takes more energy, burns more calories, and makes for a faster weight loss. Walking slowly (2 mph) takes less energy, burns fewer calories, and makes for a slower weight loss.

The Walker's Simplified Weight Loss Diet

You have seen how walking alone can help you to lose weight (one pound every two and a half weeks on the every-other-day program) with no reduction of calories from your present diet.

Now, if you would like to speed up your weight-reduction program, you can follow this simple, effective two-step formula and lose an additional half-pound, one pound or two pounds a week, by reducing your intake of calories.

Step 1

Estimate your ideal body weight (the weight you would like to be). You can do this by using a simple formula:

66

Males—106 pounds for the first five feet in height, plus six pounds for each additional inch.
Example: 5′9″ = 160 lbs.

Females—100 pounds for the first five feet in height, plus five pounds for each additional inch.
Example: 5′2″ = 110 lbs.

Step 2

Find your present weight on the following chart (Table III). The first column shows the number of calories you consume daily to maintain your present weight. The next three columns show the number of calories you will have to consume daily if you wish to lose half a pound, one pound or two pounds per week.

Table III

Weight	Number of calories per day necessary to:		
	Maintain	Lose	Lose	Lose
Females	Pres. wt.	½ lb./wk.	1 lb./wk.	2 lbs./wk.
110	1700	1450	1200	700
120	1800	1550	1300	800
130	1900	1650	1400	900
140	2000	1750	1500	1000
150	2100	1850	1600	1100
160	2300	2050	1800	1300
170	2400	2150	1900	1400
180	2500	2250	2000	1500
190	2600	2350	2100	1600
200	2700	2450	2200	1700

Males	Maintain Pres. wt.	Lose ½ lb./wk.	Lose 1 lb./wk.	Lose 2 lbs./wk.
130	2300	2050	1800	1300
140	2400	2150	1900	1400
150	2500	2250	2000	1500
160	2700	2450	2200	1700
170	2800	2550	2300	1800
180	2900	2650	2400	1900
190	3100	2850	2600	2100
200	3200	2950	2700	2200
210	3300	3050	2800	2300
220	3400	3150	2900	2400

The Walker's Simplified Diet offers a weight-reduction plan that is easy and flexible. You don't have to give up forever any of the major food groups, and you don't have to endure meals of a monotonous sameness.

You can plan your own menus by (1) consulting Appendix I for the caloric values of various foods and (2) being aware of the nutritional content of these foods.

By following the guidelines given below, you will have a diet that is properly balanced, with the correct radio of protein, carbohydrate, fat, minerals and vitamins. This is essential for good nutrition.

Whether you are reducing or maintaining your weight, your diet should include:

fresh fruits
fresh vegetables
lean meats
fish
fowl
enriched bread
fortified whole-grain cereals
low-fat dairy products

Avoid:
fried/fatty foods
sweets (candy, cake, ice cream, chocolate,
   most desserts)
sweetened soft drinks
alcoholic beverages
canned fruits in syrups
gravy and sauces
creamed soups
rich salad dressings
processed snack foods
most refined sugar/flour products
excessive use of salt

Finally, avoid the temptation to speed things up by "crash dieting," prolonged fasting or fad dieting. By depriving your body of major nutrients, you could be taking chances with your health.

Maintenance

Once you have reached your desired weight, you can keep the scale reading just where you want it by keeping your caloric intake at the maintenance number for your weight (Table III).

Find the maintenance number of calories per day (in the first column) for your present weight. Then remember to add 200 calories to this number (your 200-calorie bonus for walking). The total is the number of calories you need every day to keep your weight stable.

"Spot" Weight-loss Walking

With most weight-reduction programs, there is no allowance for human frailty. You know you're not supposed to have a slice of pizza. But you want it—desperately. You've been pretty conscientious about eating the right foods, so just this once, you succumb to temptation.

If you're an intelligent, determined dieter, you accept the lapse. With some very rigid regimens, one slipup sometimes sends the dieter into a "guilt fit," a "what's the use" mood that triggers a major eating binge.

With your walking program, you have a built-in safety valve, a way you can indulge an occasional weakness without feeling like you've taken the first step back to fatness.

If you absolutely can't live without some ice cream, then have it—just this once. And walk an extra 35 minutes to get rid of the extra calories you've picked up. No harm done.

The following table will give you an idea of how many minutes of walking at the moderate pace (3 mph) are necessary to burn up the caloric values of some common foods:

Table IV

apple (large)	20 minutes
bacon (2 slices)	19 minutes
banana (medium)	18 minutes
beer (8 oz.)	22 minutes
bread (1 slice)	12 minutes
cake (1 slice)	60 minutes
cereal (½ cup with milk)	32 minutes
chicken (fried, 1 piece)	42 minutes
donut	30 minutes
egg (1, boiled)	15 minutes
hamburger	70 minutes
ice cream (1 serving)	35 minutes
malted milk shake	100 minutes

milk (1 glass)	33 minutes
orange (medium)	15 minutes
pie (1 slice)	75 minutes
pizza (1 slice)	38 minutes
soda (8 oz.)	21 minutes
spaghetti (1 portion)	75 minutes
steak (4 oz.)	50 minutes

To calculate the walking time needed to burn off the caloric value of other foods, just check Appendix I for the item in question and divide by five. This calculation is based on the fact that walking at a moderate pace expends about five calories per minute. Example:

large apple = 100 calories ÷ 5 cal/min = 20 minutes

glass of whole milk = 160 calories ÷ 5 cal/min = 32 minutes

9

BEFORE YOU START

Wings for the angels, but feet for men
—JOSIAH GILBERT HOLLAND

Although walking doesn't produce the same strains that more intense activities do on your body, it is still important to have a complete physical examination before you begin any exercise program.

The examination will probably include a careful medical history, a resting electrocardiogram, a chest X-ray, blood tests and a urinalysis. For some people, especially those over 40, the physician may recommend an exercise electrocardiogram. This test is performed on a treadmill. It measures the activity of the heart while it is beating forcefully. While the exercise electrocardiogram doesn't always rule out the possibility of heart disease, it does give your doctor the information he needs to recommend a safe level of physical activity.

After you get the green light from your doctor, familiarize yourself with these basic rules for the walker. They will make your exercise program safe, pleasant and effective.

73

General tips

1. If you experience chest pain, excessive fatigue, dizziness, shortness of breath or pain and discomfort anywhere in your body, see your doctor immediately, before you resume walking.

2. If you have a medical condition that requires medication or treatment (high blood pressure or diabetes, for example), check with your doctor before starting on any walking program.

3. Avoid walking immediately after meals. Give yourself time to digest your food.

4. Maintain proper weight. If you have a problem in this area, refer to Chapter 8.

5. Avoid walking outdoors in extremes of cold or heat and when the humidity is high.

6. Do not smoke, since carbon monoxide buildup decreases the delivery of oxygen to the tissues, and nicotine narrows the blood vessels, further impairing the circulation.

7. Walk every other day (more if you like) to maintain maximal physical conditioning.

8. Limit your alcohol consumption, since it has an adverse effect on the heart and on your capability to exercise.

9. Heart rate should not exceed 90–110 beats per minute (depending on your age). Remember—*any walking program at any speed is beneficial.*

10. If you become tired, stop and rest. Four 15-minute sessions or three 20-minute sessions daily are just as effective as a continuous one-hour walk.

What do you need?

One of the great things about walking is that

you don't have to spend a fortune on fancy gear. But if you are one of those people who feel motivated by a colorful warmup suit or a jazzy pair of running shoes, then by all means indulge yourself.

Since you will need some way of calculating time and distance, you might want to invest some money in a pedometer. A finely calibrated pedometer, designed especially for walking, costs about $15; a multipurpose version, suitable either for running or walking, costs a few dollars less.

The pedometer is a small instrument that looks like a watch, attaches to your belt or pocket, and measures how far you walk in a given amount of time. Its mechanism depends on an oscillating weight that causes the dial to advance a certain distance with each step. All you have to do is set the stride-length adjustment on the pedometer and walk at a steady, even pace. The distance you walk is then recorded on the dial.

If you are going to do any of your walking after sunset, on country or suburban roads, it's a good idea to get some light-reflective tape for your jacket or sweater. Or you can buy one of those strap-on safety lights used by cyclists.

Feet: The "Cinderellas" of the Body

Although you don't need fancy or special shoes, you must take proper care of your feet. In the average lifetime, a pair of feet will take their owner a distance equal to two and a half trips around the world. They work hard, day in and day out, but the reward for all this faithful service is usually indifference and neglect.

A woman may cream her face and soothe her hands with lotions; a man will splash after-shave on his face and blow-dry his hair. But both are likely to pay little attention to their feet—unless they hurt.

Though feet are not as visible as hair, lips or eyes, they are important. Each foot is a very complex structure consisting of 26 bones, 56 ligaments, 38 muscles and four arches.

Feet carry the entire weight of the body, hold it in an upright position and maintain its balance while you walk.

Since the feet are the farthest distance from the heart, the circulation there tends to decrease, especially with age.

Day after day, they take a beating. In their constant pounding on hard surfaces, they absorb shock and become vulnerable to injury. To add insult to injury, they spend the day encased in shoes and socks, in a hot and sweaty atmosphere that stimulates the growth of fungi and bacteria.

Since your feet are going to do most of the work in your walking program, the least you can do is liberate them from their "Cinderella" status and keep them comfortable and healthy.

Foot Care

1. Wash feet daily with warm (not hot) water and a mild soap. Dry carefully, especially between the toes.

2. If your feet are hot and sweaty, you may want to give them a little extra treatment. After washing with warm, soapy water, rinse with cool water and elevate the feet for 15 minutes or a half-hour. Rinse again with cool water, dry thoroughly and dust with baby powder or cornstarch.

3. For feet that are dry and flaky, wash in

the usual way. After drying, apply a rich moisturizing cream or lotion, preferably before going to bed.

4. To avoid the formation of blisters or calluses, wear soft, clean, loose-fitting socks or stockings that are free of holes, bumpy spots or darns. Choose white, preferably cotton, whenever possible.

5. Toenails should be cut straight across the top, never down into the nail grooves. An emery board may be preferable to a pair of scissors.

6. If you develop excessive blisters, calluses, corns, bunions or ingrown toenails that persist or interfere with your walking program, report to your physician. Do not attempt to perform any minor surgery or treat these conditions on your own.

7. Avoid tight-fitting garments such as stockings, socks and garters with elastic bands; these can reduce the circulation to your feet.

8. Avoid the use of heating pads or hot water bottles, as they may impair circulation.

9. Avoid prolonged sitting, especially with the legs crossed, since this, too, can reduce circulation to the legs.

10. If you experience cramping pain and numbness in your feet and legs during walking, and if this pain is relieved by rest, see your doctor. You may be suffering from a condition known as *intermittent claudication* (decreased circulation to the legs).

11. Dress warmly in winter and comfortably in summer, since extremes in temperature can impair the circulation in your legs.

12. Avoid tobacco in any form. Nicotine constricts (narrows) the blood vessels and may

77

cause impaired circulation. Smoking also causes a buildup of carbon monoxide in the blood, a condition which further decreases the amount of oxygen carried to the legs.

13. When your feet are tired, soothe them by soaking alternately in warm, then cold water. Elevate for greater relaxation (the Japanese, for example, traditionally place their feet on pillows at night).

14. To stretch your heel cords, walk on bare heels for a few minutes each day, as long as this causes no discomfort.

15. Exercise your feet by flexing and extending the toes. When the weather is warm, walk barefoot on the beach.

Shoes for Walking

If you're one of those people who enjoys shopping in athletic shops and sporting goods stores, then you might want to treat yourself to a pair of good running/walking shoes, made by companies like Nike or Brooks or Adidas. If your approach to footwear is strictly functional, that's fine, too. Just keep the following checkpoints in mind:

1. Wear a properly fitted, low-heeled shoe for maximum comfort and safety. Whatever the style, be very careful about the fit. It has been estimated that about 87 percent of all Americans have foot problems, most of which are caused by ill-fitting shoes. These problems can include not only corns, bunions and blisters, but also backaches and leg cramps. Shoes should be at least a quarter-inch longer than your longest toe. Since one foot is often longer than the other, buy the larger size. Don't try to stretch shoes to fit; it's better to use shoe pads to tighten up the fit for the smaller foot.

2. Don't automatically buy the same shoe size you bought before. Although your feet generally stop growing at about age 18, a change in weight or different exercise patterns can alter your measurements. Try before you buy.

3. Don't buy shoes at the beginning of the day or at the end, when your feet have fully expanded. Do not make allowances for shoes that are almost comfortable. (Pay no attention to salesmen who promise that "these will be fine after you've broken them in.") Shoes should feel good from the moment you put them on. Don't be afraid to take your time and test by wiggling your toes. The heel should fit closely, and the arch must be the same length as your own.

4. The toe section should be wide and high enough not to cause compression of your toes.

5. The shank (section between the heel and ball of your foot) should be wide enough to fit the bottom of your foot comfortably.

6. The uppers (part of the shoe above the sole) should be soft and flexible enough to bend with your foot. Soft leather, fabrics and suedes are good. Avoid synthetic (man-made) materials, such as vinyl and patent leather, since they are not porous or flexible.

7. The sole and heel of the shoe should be made of thick rubber—waffle, ripple or standard crepe. These are all safer and less likely to slip than synthetic materials. Crepe soles are the most practical for everyday use, since they are the most durable. They are well cushioned, resilient and extremely comfortable because they can absorb some of the shock your foot encounters when you walk on a hard surface.

6. Sneakers, tennis shoes or running shoes

should have a wide, high, flexible toe box. This allows enough space to prevent crowding of the toes, which can result in toe and nail injuries. If you choose this type of shoe, be careful that it provides good support and adequate cushioning for your foot.

7. Avoid walking in high heels, which cause the foot to slide forward and increase the possibility of corns, bunions and even hammertoes. Continual use of high heels can shorten your Achilles tendons, making them more susceptible to injury.

8. Avoid boots with extremely high heels, since they prevent stability in walking. These boots are often designed to fit tightly around the leg. They can cut off the circulation and cause inflammation of the veins in the calves.

9. Avoid high platforms and clogs. They often cause ankle and foot injuries and, on occasion, painful bleeding under the toenails.

10. A solid oxford type of shoe is especially well designed for walking. Hiking shoes or boots are also excellent, but they are not really necessary unless you plan to walk over rough terrain.

10

HOW, WHEN AND WHERE

Johann Hurlinger of Austria walked from Vienna to Paris in 1900—on his hands
—THE LESLIE FREWIN BOOK OF RIDICULOUS FACTS

The Heel-Toe Method

For the most comfortable walking position, start with your weight over your feet—or just slightly ahead of them. Your body should be relaxed, with the knees slightly bent. Take easy, relaxed steps, in a regular, even stride.

To use the leg muscles most efficiently (and thus increase the circulation to these muscles), use the "heel-toe method" (Figure 13), pointing the feet straight ahead. Bring the leading leg forward, in front of the body, and allow the heel of the leading foot to touch the ground, just before the ball of the foot and the toes.

Shift your weight forward as the knee is bent, so that the heel is raised and the toes can push off to the next step. If your arms and shoulders are relaxed, they will swing almost automatically with each stride. No other special arm action or force is needed.

Keep your posture erect, with shoulders loose and arms carried low. If you hold your arms too high, you'll create fatigue and tension in your neck and shoulder muscles.

Walk at a brisk (about 3 mph), not a fast (4 mph) pace. You will notice that your breathing will automatically become slightly faster and deeper. But if you feel short of breath, you're walking too fast. It's not necessary—or wise—to punish yourself when you start an exercise program. Listen to your body. When you're tired—stop. Then resume walking after you feel rested.

Walk smoothly, putting energy into each step. You will begin to feel relaxed and loose, as your stride becomes natural and effortless. After you have been walking awhile, you will begin to develop your own rhythm and a pleasant feeling of near-weightlessness. The stride that is most natural for your weight and height will become automatic. As you use your body in this perfect exercise, you will lose any feeling of fatigue you might have and experience instead a sense of buoyancy and exhilaration.

Walking Cycle

During the gait cycle of walking, there is a brief moment when both feet support the body at the same time (bipedal stance)—followed by one-foot support (unipedal) during midstance. This is followed again by the bipedal stance at toe-off (Figure 14).

The walker uses a wider gait than does the runner. This wider gait gives greater stability as you walk. It means that you use less muscular activity to support your body, and it is the reason you can walk long distances without tiring, and with less likelihood of injuries.

Figure 13

How to walk properly

To get the most out of your walking program, walk with the heel-and-toe method. Proper walking uses calf muscles more productively and improves blood flow to these muscles. The diagram below explains heel-and-toe walking.

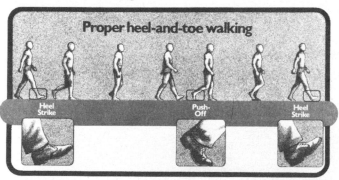

Proper heel-and-toe walking

Heel Strike — Push-Off — Heel Strike

Heel Strike:	Push-Off:	Heel Strike:
Heel of leading foot touches the floor before the ball of the foot and toes.	Knee is bent so heel is raised; weight is shifted forward. (This is essential and you should feel the action in the calf muscles.) Toes push off to next step.	Leg is accelerated forward to get in front of body. Foot is positioned for next heel strike.

Figure 14

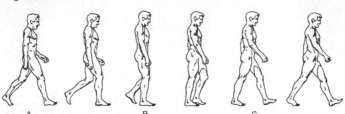

A   B   C

In walking there is a period of bipedal stance at heel contact (A), followed by a unipedal support during midstance (B), and again followed by bipedal stance at toe-off (C).

Reproduced with permission of *The Physician's Sportsmedicine,* published by McGraw-Hill, Inc., from an article by Steven I. Subotnick, D.P.M., M.S., April, 1979.   Illustration: Fred Dingler

Where and When

In the early stages of your walking program, choose places that are relatively flat. For a beginner, hills create too much stress and strain on the cardiovascular and musculo-skeletal systems.

Later, after you've completed your six weeks' conditioning, you can expand your horizons. If you have a taste for adventure, you can set your sights on the kind of walking tours favored by Gary Moore. In 1977, he walked across America. The following year, he began a 3000-mile trek that took him from Texas to Panama, through the jungles of Guatemala and the war zones of Nicaragua. Moore averaged about 20 miles a day—and wore out a pair of shoes every 600 miles.

Even if this seems a bit ambitious, there's no reason why every walker can't have some fun and adventure. Keeping in mind that *regularity* is the keystone of a successful exercise program, find a way to integrate walking into your life. And choose a way that you can anticipate with some pleasure—at least some of the time—the way you would a nice coffee break. When exercise, no matter how beneficial, becomes a dreaded chore, it is certain to have a very short-term existence in your life. The trap to avoid is the everything-that's-good-for-you-must-be-a-drag syndrome.

While you alone can best decide the "when and where" of your walking program, here are a few general suggestions to help you get started:

1. If you work at home, take pick-me-up walks at a time when physical and mental energies are starting to flag, during late-morning and/or late-afternoon hours, for example.

2. If you live a reasonable (for you) distance from work, make the trip back and forth on foot.

3. If the distances between home and work are too great, drive to a convenient location a half-mile or a mile from your destination.

4. If you use public transportation, get off a few stops ahead of your normal station and walk the rest of the way.

5. If you're an early riser, you can schedule your walks before breakfast and/or before dinner.

6. If you have formal coffee breaks at your place of work, skip the Danish or muffin, and take a "walking break" instead.

7. If you have an hour for lunch, use half the time for walking. The physiological tonic you get from walking, combined with the shortened lunch hour, will make it easier for you to skip gooey desserts.

8. If you do a lot of air travel, plan to do some of your walking in the broad expanses of airline terminals.

9. If the weather is bad, walk in an enclosed mall or shopping center.

10. If you're a woman who normally wears high heels to work, keep a pair of low-heeled shoes handy, so you can take advantage of good weather or free time whenever you have it.

Weekend walking trips can be more elaborate and more leisurely. For the individual who works at a pressure-cooker job all week, a Sunday walk in pleasant surroundings can be an excellent way to "wind down"—much better than the competitive games that exchange one kind of tension for another. For couples, a long weekend walk can be a way of beating the we-never-have-time-to-talk syndrome that afflicts so many relationships. No matter how busy you are during the week, a few shared hours at the end of it—walking and talking on a country road or a pretty street—can be great medicine, for the soul as well as for the body. For families, walking trips can be a way of establishing a lifetime of healthy habits, of fostering a natural "togetherness"—and of beating the ridiculous costs of conventional entertainment. If your children are already addicted to television, movies and sporting events for their weekend recreation, you may have to sweeten your offer of a walk with a familiar treat. But once you've enjoyed together the pleasure of self-reliance, the absence of artificial stimulation, the freedom from bus schedules, movie schedules and gas lines, you'll probably find that you've established a popular family tradition.

Almost every area will have some attractions around which you can build a walking trip. If you live in the country or near a beach, plan a walk that will take you to a favorite spot, or to one you've been wanting to explore. If you like, enjoy a picnic or a thermos of coffee or lemonade before you head back (note: if you do have a meal, rest awhile before you begin walking again). If you're interested in photography, bird-watching or amateur archaeology, walking can add another dimension to your hobbies.

If you live in the city, walking will allow you to explore and appreciate your surroundings in a way that you never could, tied to the wheels of a car or bus. Every city offers guide books or maps showing points of interest. Use one of these—or chart your own itinerary. Choose one or more destinations that appeal most to you: a museum, an art gallery, a historic shrine, an amusement park, a restaurant or the downtown shopping district—whatever will be fun.

When you run out of places to explore, drive to the next town, park your car—and start all over again. Actually, you can get a lot of walking mileage out of any area, because just as various places start to seem too familiar, the seasons will change, and your surroundings will take on a different quality.

Should you decide to branch out even further, there are a number of organizations that promote walking (see Appendix II). Even if you're not ready for a walk across the country, you and your family might enjoy a city- or statewide walking vacation.

Weather Conditions

Walking can be done safely in many kinds of weather. You don't need blue skies and sunshine every day. If you have an umbrella and raincoat

87

handy, the smell and feeling of a light rain can be a refreshing change from your indoor routine.

However, I do give my patients some general "do's" and "don'ts" regarding the weather. The most important single rule is to avoid physical exertion when the humidity is high or when the day is extremely hot, cold or windy. When the outside temperature is above 75 degrees F., or when the humidity is much above 50 percent, your body may not be able to cool itself quickly enough to avoid danger to your health.

As you exercise, you expend energy and produce heat. The only effective way to get rid of that heat is to perspire and then have that perspiration evaporate from the body's surface. Obviously, high temperatures and high humidity are going to interfere with this process, and cause the body temperature to go up. Even if you take in enough fluids before and after exercise in hot weather, you still create a strain—and a risk—to your cardiovascular system.

When the weather is hot and muggy, take your walk in the early morning or late evening—and avoid most of the problems associated with high temperatures, high humidity and radiant-heat exposure.

Extremely cold or windy weather can also be problematic, since it produces strain on the lungs and heart. If you must be outdoors in this kind of weather, dress warmly and cover exposed surfaces (mouth, ears, nose, hands, feet) to guard against frostbite.

Be careful, too, at high altitudes, since there is a decrease in the oxygen content of the air—which, in turn, can affect your response to physical activity. Because the blood transports less oxygen to the muscles, fatigue sets in more rapidly during exercise. If you have a preexisting heart or lung condition, if you develop difficulty in breathing, or if you tire easily under normal circumstances, be especially careful at high altitudes. If you have none of these conditions, a bit of routine caution will insure freedom from problems.

Indoor Exercise

Once you've launched your walking program, what will you do when the weather is bad enough to keep you indoors? You can, as we mentioned before, walk in covered areas. Or you can keep up your exercise schedule in your own home.

A stationary bike is a good walking substitute, and you don't have to make a big cash investment to get one. If you own any kind of bicycle, you can convert it into a stationary bike by buying a "rear bike wheel converter" at any sporting goods or bicycle store. This takes no special skills to attach and remove.

If you pedal at a comfortable rate (equivalent to 6–8 miles per hour), you can equal your daily walking requirements in half an hour. You can also break this up into three ten-minute sessions, to avoid fatigue and/or boredom.

If you don't own a bicycle, you can walk in place (this was a favorite exercise in elementary school gym classes, especially when there was a shortage of athletic equipment). Simply move your arms briskly and lift each leg about two or three inches from the ground. A rate of 50–60 steps per minute (count only when your right foot hits the ground) allows you to finish the day's walking in 20 minutes. You can break this up into four five-minute sessions if you like.

While both of these substitutes can be boring, they can be done as you watch television, listen to music, visit with a friend or read. When the weather is really unpleasant, the controlled climate conditions indoors and the satisfaction of keeping up your exercise program without interruption can compensate for the occasional dullness of walking substitutes.

Time and Distance

Many exercise programs are too complicated. They require special equipment, a specific location and time, and athletic ability. With walking, all you need are comfortable clothes, appropriate shoes and a way to measure approximate distances.

Using the odometer of a bike or automobile, measure the distance between two familiar points. Then you can use this information to make estimates of distance in the same area on foot.

In many cities, twenty blocks equal one mile. So if you walk around one square block five times, you will have walked one mile. This distance isn't uniform from city to city, but you can check any local variations with your street department.

For more precise measurements of distance, you can use any one of these three methods:

I. *Steps/Minute*

You can calculate the distance you walk in any given time by counting the number of steps you take in one minute at your normal walking speed. Then consult the following chart, which is based on the average stride (two feet per step). Since there are 5,280 feet per mile, it will take 2,640 steps to walk one mile. Refer to the step/minute column, and find the number closest to the number of steps you take per minute. You will then have the approximate time it will take you to walk one mile.

Table V

Steps/Mile	Steps/Minute	Distance walked	Time
(2-foot stride)			
2,640	44	1 mile	60 min.
2,640	48	1 mile	55 min.
2,640	53	1 mile	50 min.
2,640	59	1 mile	45 min.
2,640	66	1 mile	40 min.
2,640	75	1 mile	35 min.
2,640	88	1 mile	30 min.
2,640	106	1 mile	25 min.
2,640	132	1 mile	20 min.
2,640	176	1 mile	15 min.

Note: This chart will vary slightly, depending on the length of your stride. To determine your stride length (in feet), measure the distance from toe to toe or heel to heel.

II. *Walking Pace*

An even simpler method refers to the following schedule. This chart is based on the three most common walking speeds, measured in miles per hour: slow (2 mph), moderate (3 mph) and fast (4 mph). The pace that most of us use in brisk walking is the moderate pace.

Table VI

Distance	Slow pace	Moderate pace	Fast pace
	2 mph	3 mph	4 mph
½ mile	15 min.	10 min.	7½ min.
1 mile	30 min.	20 min.	15 min.
1½ miles	45 min.	30 min.	22½ min.

Distance	Slow pace	Moderate pace	Fast pace
2 miles	60 min.	40 min.	30 min.
2½ miles	75 min.	50 min.	37½ min.
3 miles	90 min.	60 min.	45 min.

Example: Take a 30-minute walk and mark off the approximate distance you've walked. If you covered one mile, then you walk at a pace of 2 mph. If you walked a distance of one and a half miles, then your pace is 3 mph. As you will note in the section on "The Every Other Day Program," the speed of walking and the actual distance walked are not very important.

III. *Pedometer*

This is probably the easiest method for calculating the distances you walk. If you are really serious about your walking program, a pedometer can help make it fun. As your conditioning program progresses and your physical fitness improves, you will be pleasantly surprised to see how quickly and easily the miles accumulate on this instrument.

The Every Other Day Program

While most exercise programs—those for fitness training and for cardiac rehabilitation—have a high dropout rate, regular walkers tend to continue their regimens. One of the many reasons is that a walking program is flexible. However, in the beginning, it is a good idea to choose a special time on specific days of the week, just to create a pattern of regularity and consistency. Once you have started, you can easily vary the sample schedule illustrated in the following chart.

To avoid the kind of rigidity that some people find monotonous (especially at the beginning), I have developed the *Every Other Day* (or four-days-a-week) *Program*. You can decide which four days would be most convenient for you. For purposes of illustration, I have chosen Monday, Wednesday, Friday and Sunday.

The chart includes both the slow and moderate pace for the conditioning program, the first six weeks. It isn't important which pace you choose, as long as you are comfortable—and consistent—in the time you walk every day. In fact, you may find that your pace (miles per hour) falls somewhere between two rates (slow and moderate, for example). This is perfectly acceptable, since your program will be based on regularity and consistency, not on speed. I have deliberately left out the fast-paced walk, since a speed of four miles per hour is too exhausting and demanding for most people. Furthermore, it is not suitable for a lifetime walking program.

Your six-week conditioning program begins with a fifteen-minute walk every other day for the first two weeks. For the third and fourth weeks, you will take thirty-minute walks; for the last two weeks, forty-five-minute walks.

As you near the end of the six weeks, you will notice changes related to your improved aerobic capacity (the uptake and distribution of oxygen throughout the body). Among the benefits in store for you are a general feeling of well-being, less tension, improved breathing capacity, more energy and better muscle tone.

Table VII: Every Other Day Walking Program

I. Six-Week Conditioning Schedule

Day	Time	Slow pace (2 mph) Distance	Moderate pace (3 mph) Distance
1st Mon.	15 min.	½ mile	¾ mile
1st Wed.	15 min.	½ mile	¾ mile

Day	Time	Slow pace (2 mph) Distance	Moderate pace (3 mph) Distance
1st Fri.	15 min.	½ mile	¾ mile
1st Sun.	15 min.	½ mile	¾ mile
2nd Mon.	15 min.	½ mile	¾ mile
2nd Wed.	15 min.	½ mile	¾ mile
2nd Fri.	15 min.	½ mile	¾ mile
2nd Sun.	15 min.	½ mile	¾ mile
3rd Mon.	30 min.	1 mile	1½ miles
3rd Wed.	30 min.	1 mile	1½ miles
3rd Fri.	30 min.	1 mile	1½ miles
3rd Sun.	30 min.	1 mile	1½ miles
4th Mon.	30 min.	1 mile	1½ miles
4th Wed.	30 min.	1 mile	1½ miles
4th Fri.	30 min.	1 mile	1½ miles
4th Sun.	30 min.	1 mile	1½ miles
5th Mon.	45 min.	1½ miles	2¼ miles
5th Wed.	45 min.	1½ miles	2¼ miles
5th Fri.	45 min.	1½ miles	2¼ miles
5th Sun.	45 min.	1½ miles	2¼ miles
6th Mon.	45 min.	1½ miles	2¼ miles
6th Wed.	45 min.	1½ miles	2¼ miles
6th Fri.	45 min.	1½ miles	2¼ miles
6th Sun.	45 min.	1½ miles	2¼ miles

To get the greatest benefits from your program, you should next work up to a regular maintenance schedule of one hour every other day—or any four days of the week you choose.

How far should you walk during this hour? Again—don't worry. It's the time you walk, and not the distance, which is most important. Whether you walk two, two and one half or three miles during the

94

hour, you will continue to gain psychological and physiological benefits.

Table VIII

II. Maintenance schedule

Day	Time	Slow pace (2 mph) Distance	Moderate pace (3 mph) Distance
Every Mon.	60 min.	2 miles	3 miles
Every Wed.	60 min.	2 miles	3 miles
Every Fri.	60 min.	2 miles	3 miles
Every Sun.	60 min.	2 miles	3 miles

Remember—you don't have to spend your hour all at once. Think of it as a dollar bill. If small change is more practical for you, cash it in for smaller amounts. For example: fifteen minutes morning and evening, to and from work, and a half-hour at lunchtime add up to the same results as one full hour at a time. If it's easier to walk a half-hour every day, instead of an hour every other day, that's fine, too. For best results, however, try not to make any session shorter than fifteen minutes. As long as you walk consistently, the benefits are the same, so take advantage of the flexibility that can make walking a convenient part of anyone's busy day.

A Record of Your Walking Program

Keep your daily walking record on the chart below. In the boxes marked *Time*, enter the time you walked on that particular day. In the boxes marked *Distance*, enter the approximate distance you walked on that day.

Continue the record for at least twelve weeks—the six weeks' conditioning program and the first six weeks of your maintenance program—until walking becomes an automatic part of your life, like brushing your teeth and washing your face. Record the times and distances actually walked.

Make every effort to follow your chosen schedules—but remember they are only guidelines. Enjoy flexibility, but never walk less than three days (four are preferable) in any given week.

Table IX

Example:

Week	Mon.	Tues.	Wed.	Thurs.	Fri.	Sat.	Sun.
1 Time	10 min.		12 min.		15 min.		15 min.
Distance ¼ mi.			¼ mi.		½ mi.		½ mi.
2 Time		15 min.		15 min.		20 min.	
Distance		½ mi.		½ mi.		¾ mi.	

Walking Program Record

Week	Mon.	Tues.	Wed.	Thurs.	Fri.	Sat.	Sun.
1 T							
D							
2 T							
D							
3 T							
D							
4 T							
D							
5 T							
D							
6 T							

D

7 T

D

8 T

D

9 T

D

10 T

D

11 T

D

12 T

D

APPENDIX I

Caloric Values

Abbreviations: av. = average, c. = cup, lg. = large, med. = medium, pc. = piece, sl. = slice, sm. = small, sq. = square, sv. = serving, t. = teaspoon, T. = tablespoon

BEVERAGES Calories

Beer 12 oz. glass 1	180	Gin 1 ounce	70
Brandy 1 ounce	100	Lemonade 1 c.	100
Buttermilk 1 c.	80	Malted milk 1 c.	200
Cola 12 oz. bottle	160	Malted milk choc.	
Cocoa with milk		1 c.	350
1 c.	180	Manhattan 1	160
Coffee, black 1 c.	0	Martini 1	150
Coffee 1 T. cream		Milk, evaporated	
1 c.	50	1 c.	320
Coffee 2 t. sugar		Milk, skim 1 c.	90
1 c.	50	Milk, whole 1 c.	170
Cream, thin 2 T.	60	Old Fashioned 1	150
Cream, thick 2 T.	100	Rum 1 ounce	70
Eggnog 1 c.	230	Sherry 1 wineglass	140
Ginger ale 1 c.	75	Tea, no cream or	
		sugar	0

Whiskey 1 ounce	70	Doughnut, plain 1	120
Wine (white 85;		Fruit sm. sl.	250
red	150)	Gingerbread 2″ sq.	200

BREADS

Ginger snap 1		20
Lady fingers 1		50
Boston Brown		
sm. sl.	70	Marble 1 sl. 215
Bran 1 sl.	75	Pound 1 sl. 140
Biscuits 2 sm.	100	Sponge sm. sl. 100

Boston Brown
sm. sl. 70
Bran 1 sl. 75
Biscuits 2 sm. 100
Coffee cake
1½″ sq. 100
Corn 2 ″ x 2″ x 1″ 100
Cracker, Graham 1 35
Cracker, saltine 1 15
Dumpling 1 100
French toast 1 pc. 135
Melba toast 1 sl. 25
Muffin 1 sm. 135
Pancake 1 60
Pizza 1 sl. 250
Pretzel 5 sticks 18
Raisin 1 sl. 100
Roll, Parker
House 1 100
Roll, sweet 1 175
Rye 1 sl. 65
Waffle 1 215
White 1 sl. 65
Whole wheat 1 sl. 75
Zwieback 1 20

CAKES

Angel Food
med. sl. 150
Brownies 2″ sq. 140
Chocolate sm. sl. 200
Cupcake (plain) 150
100

Doughnut, plain 1 120
Fruit sm. sl. 250
Gingerbread 2″ sq. 200
Ginger snap 1 20
Lady fingers 1 50
Marble 1 sl. 215
Pound 1 sl. 140
Sponge sm. sl. 100

CEREALS

Bran flakes ⅔ c. 100
Cornflakes 1 c. 100
Cornmeal ¾ c. 100
Cream of Wheat
¼ c. 75
Grape-Nuts ¼ c. 115
Oatmeal ½ c. 80
Puffed Rice 1 c. 60
Rice, white ½ c. 100
Shredded Wheat 1 120
Wheaties 1 c. 135

CHEESE & EGGS

Cheese, Amer.
1″ cube 80
Cheese, cottage
¼ c. 65
Cheese, cream
¼ cake 90
Cheese, Swiss
⅛″ sl. 100
Eggs, fried 1 120
Eggs, omelet
2 eggs 250
Eggs, 1 whole 70
Eggs, scrambled
¼ c. 100

DESSERTS

Bread pudding ½ c. 150
Brown Betty ½ c. 200
Chocolate eclair 1 250
Chocolate pudding
  ½ c. 200
Chocolate soda
  1 gl. 400
Cornstarch pdg.
  ½ c. 200
Custard ⅔ c. 200
Ice cream, choc.
  ½ c. 250
Ice cream, plain
  ½ c. 200
Jello 1 c. 75
Prune whip ⅔ c. 100
Rice pudding ½ c. 200
Shortcake, fruit
  1 pc. 300
Tapioca pudding
  ½ c. 150

FRUITS

Apple, baked 1 175
Apple, raw 1 lg. 100
Applesauce ½ c. 150
Apricots, canned 6 150
Apricots, fresh 3 60
Apricots, stewed
  ½ c. 200
Banana 1 med. 100
Blackberries, fr.
  ½ c. 50
Blueberries, fr.
  ½ c. 50

Cantaloupe ½ 50
Cherries, canned
  ½ c. 100
Cherries, fresh 10 50
Cranberry sauce
  ½ c. 200
Dates 3 or 4 100
Figs, dried 1 lg. 60
Grapefruit ½ 50
Grapefruit juice
  ½ c. 70
Grape juice ½ c. 100
Grapes 20 to 25 75
Honeydew melon
  ¼ 100
Lemon juice 3 T. 15
Orange 1 70
Orange juice ½ c. 50
Peaches, canned 2 100
Peaches, fresh 1
  med. 50
Pears, canned 3 100
Pears, fresh 1 med. 95
Pineapple, canned
  1 s. 100
Pineapple, fresh
  ½ c. 60
Pineapple juice
  ½ c. 75
Plums, fresh 4 50
Prune juice ½ c. 90
Prunes, stewed 4 200
Raisins 2 T. 50
Raspberries, fr.
  ½ c. 45

Rhubarb, stewed
½ c.   100
Strawberries, fr.
½ c.   50
Tangerine 1   35
Watermelon 1 sl.
¾"   100

MEATS
Beef
Corned, av. sl.   100
Corned, hash
½ c.   100
Dried, 4 thin sl.   100
Filet, 1 sm.   250
Hamburger 1
cake   100
Heart 1 med. pc.   100
Liver med. sl.   100
Roast, lean,
av. sl.   100
Beef
Sirloin steak,
av. sl.   100
Stew with veg.
½ c.   159
Tongue, 2 sm. sl.   75
Chicken
Broiled, ½   100
Roast, av. sl.   125
Duck, med. pc.
roast   300
Frankfurter, 1   125
Goose, av. sl.
roast   300
Lamb
Chop, 1 broiled   100

MEATS, Cont.
Leg of, 1 sl. roast   100
Mutton
Leg of, 1 sl. roast   235
Pork
Bacon, 4 strips   100
Chop, 1 broiled   200
Ham, 1 sl. baked   100
Ham, 1 sl. fried   200
Roast, 2 sl.   170
Sausage, 2 med.
links   100
Spareribs, 4 ribs   150
Tenderloin, 1 pc.   200
Turkey, 1 sl. roast   100
Veal
Chop, 1 lean   100
Cutlet, 1 med.
breaded   200
Leg of, 1 sl. roast   100
Stew, 1 c.   200

MISCELLANEOUS
Almonds, 10
salted   100
Butter, 1" sq.   80
Cashew nuts, 4   100
Catsup, 1T   25
French dressing,
1T   75
Gravy, 3T thick   100
Hard sauce, 1T   100
Lard, 1T   100
Macaroni & cheese,
½ c.   150
Margarine, 1T   100

Mayonnaise, 1T	100	**SEAFOOD**	
Noodles, ½ c.	60	Clams, 12	150
Olive oil, 1T	100	Codfish cakes,	
Olives, 1 lg. green	30	2 lg.	200
Peanut butter, 1T	90	Crabmeat, ½ c.	
Peanuts, 20 salted	100	canned	75
Pecans, 6 halves	50	Haddock, av. sv.	100
Popcorn, 1 c. plain	55	Halibut, av. sv.	100
Potato chips, 9	100	Lobster, ¾ c.	
Roquefort drsng,		canned	85
1T	250	Lobster, ½ c.	
Spaghetti, ¾ c.	100	fresh	125
Walnuts, 6 halves	50	Mackerel, av. sv.	125
White cause, ¼ c.	110	Oysters, 4 lg.	50
Yeast, 1 cake	20	Perch, 3 med.	280
		Pike, av. sv.	100

PIES

Apple, ⅙ pie	330	Salmon, ½ c. canned	100
Banana cream, ⅙		Salmon, av. pc.	
pie	250	fresh	100
Berry, ⅙ pie	350	Sardines, 4 canned	100
Cherry, ⅙ pie	350	Shrimp, 10	50
Custard, ⅙ pie	350	Shrimp cocktail,	
Lemon, ⅙ pie	300	½ c.	100
Mincemeat, ⅙ pie	400	Sole, av. sv. filet	100
Peach, ⅙ pie	350	Trout, 2 brook	75
Pumpkin, ⅙ pie	250	Trout, av. sv. lake	125
Raisin, ⅙ pie	400	Tuna, ½ c. canned	100
Rhubarb, ⅙ pie	350	Whitefish, av. sv.	100

SALADS

Aspic, av. sv.	110	**SOUPS**	
Chicken, ½ c.	200	Asparagus, 1 c.	
Cole slaw, 1 c.	100	cream	200
Potato, ½ c.	200	Bean, ¾ c. navy	100
Tomato, ½ c.	30	Beef broth, 1 c.	50
Waldorf, av. sv.	100	Bouillon, 1 c. clear	25

Celery, 1 c. cream	200	Beans, ½ c. string	25
Chicken, 1 c. clear	50	Beet greens, ½ c.	30
Mushroom, 1 c.		Beets, 2 med.	45
cream	200	Broccoli, ½ c.	20
Pea, ⅔ c. cream	100	Brussels sprouts, 6	50
Spinach, ¾ c.		Cabbage, ¾ c.	
cream	100	cooked	20
Tomato, 1 c. clear	50	Cabbage, ½ c. raw	15
Tomato, 1 c.		Carrots, 4 med.	
cream	230	raw	20
Vegetable, 1 c.	100	Cauliflower, 1 c.	30

SWEETS

		Celery, 3 stalks	10
Apple butter, 1T	75	Corn, ½ c. canned	100
Caramel, 1 plain	80	Corn on cob, 1 lg.	100
Chocolate bar, 1		Cucumber, 12 sl.	10
sm.	270	Eggplant, 1 sl.	
Chocolate cream,		fried	50
1	55	Lettuce, ¼ head	15
Chocolate fudge,		Onions, ½ c.	
1″	115	cooked	40
Corn syrup 1T	85	Onions, 5 sm.	
Honey, 1T	100	green	10
Jam & jelly, 1T	60	Parsnips, ¾ c.	60
Maple syrup, 1T	70	Peas, ½ c. canned	55
Marmalade, 1T	100	Peas, ½ c. fresh	75
Marshmallows, 5	100	Peppers, 2 sm.	25
Sugar, 2t brown	35	Potato, 1 med.	
Sugar, 2t gran.	50	baked	100

VEGETABLES

		Potato, 2 sm.	
Asparagus, ½ c.		boiled	100
canned	20	Potato, ½ c.	
Asparagus, 6 stalks	15	creamed	150
Beans, ⅔ c. baked	200	Potato, ½ c.	
Beans, ½ c. lima	100	mashed	100
Beans, ½ c. navy	160	Potato, 1 lg. sweet	150
		Radishes, 5	15

Sauerkraut, ⅔ c.	25	Tomato, 1 sm.	
Sauerkraut juice,		fresh	25
½ c.	20	Tomato juice, ½ c.	25
Spinach, ¾ c.	25	Turnips, ½ c.	25
Squash, ½ c.	50	Vegetable juice,	
Tomato, 1 c.		½ c.	25
canned	50		

APPENDIX II

Organizations That Promote Walking

American Forestry Association
1319 18th Street, N.W.
Washington, D.C. 20036

Appalachian Trail Conference
P. O. Box 236
Harpers Ferry, W. Va. 25425

The Federation of Western Outdoor Clubs
512½ Boylston E. #106
Seattle, Wash. 98102

National Audubon Society
950 Third Avenue
New York, N.Y. 10022

National Campers & Hikers Association
7172 Transit Road
Buffalo, N. Y. 14221

National Wildlife Federation
1412 16th Street, N.W.
Washington, D.C. 20036

The New England Trail Conference
P.O. Box 115
West Pawlet, Vt. 05775

Sierra Club
530 Bush Street
San Francisco, Ca. 94108

Walking Association
4113 Lee Highway
Arlington, Va. 22207

Wilderness Society
1901 Pennsylvania Avenue, N.W.
Washington, D.C. 20006

A free index of topographical maps for walkers is available. For areas east of the Mississippi, write to: U.S. Geological Survey's Branch of Distribution, 1220 South Eads Street, Arlington, Va. 22202. For areas west of the Mississippi, write to: U.S. Geological Survey's Branch of Distribution, Box 25286, Federal Center, Denver, Colo. 80225.

BIBLIOGRAPHY

American College of Sports Medicine. *Guidelines for Graded Exercise Testing and Exercise Prescription*. Lea and Febiger, Philadelphia, 1975.

Apple, David F., Jr., M.D. and John D. Cantwell, M.D. *Medicine for Sport*. Yearbook Medical Publishers, Chicago, 1979.

Calder, Jean. *Walking: A Guide to Beautiful Walks and Trails in America*. William Morrow & Co., New York, 1977.

Consumer Guide Editors. *Complete Book of Walking*. Simon & Schuster, New York, 1979.

Cooper, Kenneth, M.D. *Aerobics*. M. Evans & Co., New York, 1968.

————, *The Aerobics Way*. M. Evans & Co., New York, 1977.

————, *The New Aerobics*. M. Evans & Co., New York, 1970.

Donaldson, Gerald. *The Walking Book*. Holt, Rinehart & Winston, 1979.

Dreyfack, Raymond. *The Complete Book of Walking*, Farnsworth Publishing Co., 1979.

Fletcher, Colin. *The New Complete Walker: The Joys and Techniques of Hiking and Backpacking*. Alfred A. Knopf, New York, 1976.

Gale, Bill. *The Wonderful World of Walking*. William Morrow & Co., New York, 1979.

Girl Scouts of the United States. *Let's Take a Walk: An Activity Picture Book with Group Leader's Guide*. Girl Scouts of the U.S., 1975.

Katch, F.I., M.D. and W.D. McArdle, M.D. *Nutrition, Weight Control and Exercise*. Houghton Mifflin Co., 1977.

Kinney Shoe Corporation and Wayne Barrett. *Walking Tours of America: Mini-Tours in Major Cities on Foot*. Macmillan, New York, 1979.

Man, John. *Walk! It Could Change Your Life*. Paddington Press, 1979.

Marchetti, Albert. *Dr. Marchetti's Walking Book: Getting All the Physical Benefits of Running Without Taking the Risks*. Stein & Day, 1979.

Mirkin, G., M.D. and M. Hoffman, M.D. *The Sports Medicine Book*. Little Brown & Co., Boston, 1978.

Muckle, David S., MB., B.S., F.R.C.S. *Injuries in Sport*. Yearbook Medical Publishers, Chicago, 1979.

Rudner, Ruth. *Off and Walking: A Hiker's Guide to American Places*. Holt, Rinehart & Winston, New York, 1977.

Shephard, Roy J., M.D., Ph.D. *Physical Activity and Aging*. Yearbook Medical Publishers, Chicago, 1979.

Sutton, Ann and Myron Sutton. *The Appalachian Trail: Wilderness on the Doorstep*. J.B. Lippincott, Philadelphia, 1967.

Zochert, Donald. *Walking in America*. Alfred A. Knopf, New York, 1974.

111